THE SOUL HUSTLERS

Books by Rene Noorbergen

THE SOUL HUSTLERS
PROGRAMMED TO LIVE
THE ARK FILE
CHARISMA OF THE SPIRIT
ELLEN G. WHITE—PROPHET OF DESTINY
YOU ARE PSYCHIC
JEANE DIXON—MY LIFE AND PROPHECIES

THE SOUL HUSTLERS

RENÉ NOORBERGEN

ZONDERVAN PUBLISHING HOUSE OF THE ZONDERVAN CORPORATION
GRAND RAPIDS, MICHIGAN 49506

Library of Congress Cataloging in Publication Data

Noorbergen, Rene.
  The soul hustlers.

  1. Occult sciences—Controversial literature.
2. Psychical research—Controversial literature.
3. Flying saucers—Controversial literature.
I. Title.
BF1411.N64   133'.7   76-11801

Lovingly dedicated to Judie

"And the Lord God said, It is not good
that the man should be alone; I will
make him an help meet for him."

—Genesis 2:18

Contents

One 13

INVASION FROM BEYOND

Two 45

CHECKING SATAN'S REALM

Three 63

THE ELECTRONIC PROBE

Four 99

THE DEVIL'S NAKED TRUTH

Five 113

WILL THE REAL JEANE DIXON PLEASE STAND UP?

Six 141

THE COUNTERFEIT

Seven 171

THE STARS DON'T TELL

An exposé into the hoax of astrology, the UFO mystery
that will not die, and what the psychics don't tell you

Invasion From Beyond

1

1 Invasion From Beyond

THE TIME IS 8:30 P.M. THE YEAR —
1975. The place — a sleepy town somewhere
in Kansas. The unconscious form of a lovely
young girl lies motionless on the damp
stone floor of a shallow basement room, nearly smothered by
the putrid stench of body odors emanating from a group of
loathsome hooded figures dancing about with a macabre
cadence, chanting in monotone voices.

It's hot, and the tightly shut door makes the sweltering
atmosphere even more oppressive.

Drying beads of perspiration on her head and throat
reflect a minute glimmer of the flickering flames of the drip-
ping candles that surround her tense young body, and on a
signal from the presiding priest, she is carefully lifted up and
grotesquely positioned on a black velvet cloth that covers the
rectangular natural stone altar erected in the middle of the
room. . . . Flanked by an ancient skull, a stuffed owl, and a
yellowed manuscript containing the magic rites, she has
suddenly become the focal point of a bizarre ceremony.

13

The Soul Hustlers

With a final adjustment of the black cloth, the hooded attendants withdraw and all becomes quiet. The labored breathing of the participants disappears in the vacuum of silence. Even the chilling chant has faded out. The thirteen men wait in reverent attention to hear the solemn words of dedication to be uttered by the satanic cult's high priest.

Slowly — very slowly — he moves into the magic circle and, stretching out his left arm, he positions a glistening, double-edged sword to within a hair's breath of the trembling initiate's throat. In a weird monotone he begins to chant the innokian words that are to deliver both body and soul of the cult's new member to the kingdom of Satan.

But while he intensifies his devilish ceremony, guiding it to a feverish crescendo, a group of believers of a different kind gather in New Orleans, Louisiana, all eyes focused on the face of a slightly built woman in her late fifties who has just undraped her crystal ball and is now staring intently into its shimmering depths. . . .

"Give me vision . . . give me life," she pleads quiveringly, begging for help from the powers from beyond. "Give me vision" . . . and her staring vacant eyes implore the Master of Darkness for a vision from beyond the grave to satisfy the morbid cravings of her paying customers. They sit there . . . every eye glued to the ever-changing expressions on her face.

Suddenly . . . contact! A sigh of expectation blows through the darkened room as the medium's lips begin to move and strange unfamiliar voices issuing from her white-lipped mouth clamor for attention. . . .

In still another city, a stream of well-dressed society matrons and smartly clad businessmen pour quietly into one of the city's major auditoriums, anxious to listen to the words of The Prophet. Of course, they are well aware that he is only a businessman, but his amazing degree of accuracy in predicting economic convulsions, stockmarket fluctuations, political upheavals, and even assassinations has placed him in a class by himself.

"He's a prophet, no use denying that," they whisper

among themselves in quiet admiration as his ascetic-looking figure slowly ascends the steps leading to the dimly lit podium. "He has predicted the president's assassination, hasn't he? His predictions are *accurate*, just like the Prophets of old. Even politicians and clergy agree with that. If God has given us a prophet for these troubled times, then he must be it." And while the prophet adjusts his dangling lapel microphone, his pale blue eyes searchingly scan the expectant audience, stopping momentarily with well-concealed anger at the row of empty seats in the back of the auditorium.

"What? Still people who don't believe in him? That must be changed. Better have a hard discussion with the business manager and advance man" . . . and he makes a mental note. But no one looking at his gentle, smiling face will have noticed his inner dissatisfaction and camouflaged anger, as his soft yet forceful voice begins to caress the minds of the hundreds of uplifted faces. He smiles that infectious smile of his — and they beam in return.

The prophet tells them that nothing serious will affect their lives, with the exception perhaps of the upcoming tidal wave on Florida's northeastern coast . . . "Oh yes, there's also the possibility that the next president too will be assassinated. . . . There are those vibrations, you see, that have become more intense with each passing day. Aside from that, little else will happen until 1999, when *all* will change . . ."

He pauses, and his eyes again roam the audience. There is no doubt: they are his. His words have found their mark again. A few more meetings like this one, and all the best-seller lists will show his latest book. "How gullible they are," he smiles to himself as he continues to manipulate the receptive minds, reaching for influence, for power — perhaps even the presidency itself!

Isolated cases of occult interest? Don't believe it for one moment. This interest in the occult is not spawned amid delusions of sick minds, nor does it represent ill-omened fantasies believed to have sprung from beyond the grave. If

15

this were only half true, this book might never have been written. The tragedy of it all is that the events described here are happening throughout the Western world, across the United States, in every major city, every single week of the year.

The bizarre and mysterious have always carried within themselves elements of morbid fascination. Whereas in years past it was hidden, its influence is now spreading over the hungry countryside in ever-widening circles and it is rapidly beginning to display its superstitious effects in all strata of society.

No longer is faith in the supernatural limited to the country folk who, needing sun and rain for their crops, often pleaded with the "gods of nature" for a measure of divine intervention.

"Today things are different," they say. "Science has taken the place of our former superstition." Their actions, however, belie their words, for if this is the case, *if* superstition along medieval lines has *really* left us, why do we now find the affluent of society — the doctors, the lawyers, and other upper-income-bracket individuals — lending their minds and their prestige to the extraordinary growth of modern supernatural phenomena?

The years of the Second World War were a dramatic time-period when faith in the Unknown was suppressed by the harsh reality of bombs, cannons, and the ever-lengthening breadlines — not to mention the screams of the tortured and the whimpering groans of the dying. Stark brutality ruled the masses, and only prayer provided actual help. It is not that superstition did not try to take over, but in most cases faith in God, not in the occult, furnished the necessary strength to survive.

Yet beneath it all, the supernormal continued. Astrologers on both sides of the Channel and the Atlantic Ocean influenced the decision-makers of the war. Many of Adolf Hitler's tactics resulted from precise astrological forecasts supplied him by his "court" astrologer. Day by day his modern magicians checked the stars, consulted the spirits and influenced their Fuehrer as did the astrologers of ancient Babylon. Hitler was under their control, and even Churchill was not completely devoid of supernormal persuasion.

The same weakness holds true for the statesmen of the United States. It was the Washington-based seer, Jeane Dixon, who proudly claims to recall the occasions when she was secretly summoned to the White House to advise former president Franklin Delano Roosevelt in matters of state. She even counseled him regarding his approximate time of death, she says. . . . Again, this was not uncommon, for other presidents before him had done the very same thing. The best known of these was Abraham Lincoln, whose contacts with the spiritualist medium Nettie Maynard are now almost legendary. Material in the Library of Congress tells how many of his major decisions were based on spirit guidance, supplied by disembodied voices coming from the motionless lips of Nettie Maynard. Visits to the battlefields, formulation of the Emancipation Proclamation, the establishment of the Freedman's Bureau — all were either guided by the spirits or dictated by their voices. Just because Abraham Lincoln held the highest position in the land did not necessarily make him immune from supernormal interference.

Today the Civil War is merely a red blotch on the yellowing pages of history, and even World War II has been relegated a place on the dusty shelves of the Archives. But with the lessening of the tension and travail of war, a superstitious faith in the power of supernormal events has once again assumed command. Known currently as the "Faith of the Age of Aquarius," this "new" religion has suddenly become so dynamic and so unpredictable that it is no longer realistic to speak of these modern happenings as manifestations of the occult. The very meaning of the word *occult* — "hidden phenomena," "secret arts," or simply "secret knowledge" — has lost its significance now that its fundamental principles are readily known to anyone remotely interested in these strange powers. Correspondence courses in psychic phenomena and pure Satanism are available everywhere. Witches Bibles and Satanic Bibles can be purchased at most bookstores; mediums openly promote their "contacts" in the newspapers across the country; Psychic Seminars and Satanic Pleasuredomes now dot the land. In addition, major universities have recently entered the mushrooming market for occult knowledge by offering bachelor's degrees and master's degrees in witchcraft and sorcery.

It is 1976, but the Middle Ages have invaded us once again.

What all this does to a healthy society is obvious.

These practices are not just limiting the free responses of people in general; they are *conditioning* them, *brainwashing* them, to accept all these phenomena and supernatural manifestations which were once considered to be in Satan's realm and, as such, totally unacceptable in a nominally Christian society. Some sociologists have even hinted that this might not be so detrimental after all, because this way people have something that ties them together. "Where Christianity fails," they reason, "occult sciences may succeed. It gives them something to follow." Whether this adhesive is capitalism or open Satanism is immaterial to them.

They may feel this way, but God most certainly doesn't, nor should today's Christians.

Let's face it. Supernatural manifestations have really penetrated the world of the seventies, and its workings have been widely accepted without open objection. Millions are now being deceived by this quiet faith that operates under the unassuming name of "psychic phenomena." With the alluring appeal of these mysterious occurrences, its practitioners have invaded the Christian churches. Millions the world over now proudly claim to believe in both Christianity and the occult sciences — as if that were really possible.

Because of this surging invasion of Dark Power, the statistics of this nation are rapidly undergoing dramatic changes. In the United States alone, the number of psychic believers is swelling at an unprecedented rate. Conservative estimates placed approximately 40 million Americans in the clutches of the Master of the Occult a mere four years ago. Now, in 1976, we know that this was just wishful thinking! On November 26, 1974, a startling announcement was made that should shake many Christian Americans out of their lethargy. The results of a nationwide survey conducted by the highly respected Roper Organization revealed that 53 *percent of all Americans now profess to believe in psychic phenomena and ESP.* Significant is the fact that in the class of those with incomes under $6,000 per year, 36 percent believe, while 59 percent of those with incomes of $18,000 and above believe. The statistics according to education show much the same phenomenon. Those with a high-school education score 26 percent, while 68 percent of the people with a college education believe. Startling? I think so.

Something is indeed happening to the basic beliefs of Americans. It is manifested in their church habits: while belief in psychic phenomena is on the increase, church attendance is declining. Another survey — this one published in February 1975 — reveals that education plays a meaningful role in church attendance. The statistics tell us that 45 percent of the college graduates attend church regularly, compared to 38 percent for high school graduates and 39 percent of those who have completed only grade school. With less than half of the population going to church and engaged in Christian activities, and more than half (53 percent) of Americans submitting their faith to occult powers, one might certainly ask the question whether we can still qualify even nominally for the designation "Christian" nation.

This invasion of the occult sciences has colored much of what our country does. A full 69 percent of all Americans now believe in astrology and resolutely comb the morning newspapers for their favorite astrology column, absorbing every minute detail. Does it influence our political scene? You can count on it! While many congressmen and senators do not publicly admit using astrological forecasts in their work, astrology is a big game in the nation's capital. Even local politics are affected by it. When hiring staff employees, Arrington Dixon, a District of Columbia councilman, is reported to review every applicant's astrological sign to ascertain whether the person is compatible with him and the job applied for![1] And he is no rarity.

Using the latest surveys as a guide, we know now that not just 40 million — as once believed — but 117 million Americans are currently being misled by the astrologers, the psychics, palmists, mediums, and clairvoyants. To accomplish this "total guidance," the nation's newspapers now publish no less than 1,200 daily astrology columns, while universities and major department stores draw the public to the 2,350 horoscope computers they have installed throughout the country.

How far will it go? What has been "planned" for us?

Amassing all the supernatural manifestations that are surrounding us under the general umbrella of "psychic phenomena," Jeane Dixon of Washington, D.C., says,

"Before the completion of the next decade (1970-1980), popularity of ESP and psychic phenomena will reach an all-time high. No longer will people be inhibited by what others may say about them; they will have reached the age of experimentation in psychic matters and will probe its depths to discover the power of spirituality. Many will find faith in the Lord through ESP."[2] Quite a statement coming from a practitioner of the occult!

Whereas Christianity has grown continually and has survived the murderous onslaught of nearly 2,000 years of strife and persecution, steadfastly moving onward toward the threshold of eternity, the psychic surge of today is relatively new, even though its throbbing expansion carries within it all the rudimentary knowledge of paganism dating back to the early years of man's creation. It is gray with age, but recently it has acquired a new lease on life. For exactly how long, no one knows. Both its followers and foes must agree that it has invaded major Protestant denominations with relentless force. In many cases this entry has been so phenomenal that it is beginning to replace the host church's doctrines. This is all happening because of the seemingly unquenchable desire of its practitioners to become "one with the gods," for this is the ultimate wish of those dabbling with the forces of the occult.

There are some basic differences between occult sciences and Christianity. In Christianity, the gospel teaches that there must be a *total submission* of the human mind and soul in order to elevate our being on the road to eternity. Occult believers, on the other hand, do not at all advocate *submission* to God or even to what they call a "higher power." They do not believe in submission, but rather in *cooperation with higher powers on an equal basis.* They freely concur that it is not necessarily the Christian God they want to deal with — the unknown entities residing in the mysterious abode of the spirit world will do just as well.

Underlying it all is a controversy older than the world itself. It is the result of the biblically reported battle between Christ and Satan and the controversy which is said to have shocked the entire universe (Isaiah 14; Ezekiel 28).

Among theologians and historians as well as ardent students of mythology, the conviction is gaining that the space age is much more than merely a period in which hydrogen bombs are political baby-sitters and travel to the moon is already a matter of history. It is an age in which international conflicts are still decided on the battlefields, regardless of the utopian dreams of the United Nations. It is an age of controversy and hostility, conquest and eradication; yet now more than ever before, the very survival of Christianity seems to be at stake. Today it is realistic to refer to what's happening as a desperate, agonizing battle between the forces of good and evil — that is, provided we are prepared to concede that the occult phenomena are indeed treacherous manifestations of the forces of evil. If we are not, the occult practitioners of today will readily supply the evidence necessary to convince us.

Nearly ninety years ago, one of the leaders of the spirit-guide movement, J. J. Morse, already admitted this in his book *Practical Occultism*. Said he, "Shall we come down to the plain simple truth that the phenomenal aspects of modern spiritualism reproduce all the essential principles of the Magic, Witchcraft and Sorcery of the past? The same powers are involved. . . . the same intelligences are operating."

What he really had in mind when speaking of the "essential principles" became undeniably clear twenty-six years later, when in 1914 the National Spiritualist Association of Churches defined the ways in which "their" spirit power manifests itself.

It was quite a list. And the further we progress in time, the more revealing the list becomes. This is the way it reads:

"The phenomena of spiritualism consists of *Prophecy, Clairvoyance, Gift of Tongues, Laying on of Hands, Healing, Visions, Trance, Levitation, Raps, Automatic and Independent Writings, Painting, Voice, Materialization* [thought], *Photography, Psychometry.*"

Alarming without a doubt, for many of these phenomena are now guiding millions of people, and what's worse, only a mere handful regard them as evil.

Some critics of Christianity maintain that the Bible is an outdated book and contains nothing relevant for us, the people of the twentieth century. How mistaken they are! Most likely they are unaware that the Bible records its own list of phenomena exhibited by the psychic practitioners and submits God's own evaluation of both these practices and those who use them.

Found in Deuteronomy 18:9-12, it is a devastating judgment: " . . . Thou shalt not learn to do after the abominations of those nations. There shall not be found among you any one . . . that useth divination [fortune-telling], or an observer of times [astrologer], or an enchanter [magician], or a witch, or a charmer, or a consulter with familiar spirits [a medium who uses a spirit guide], or a wizard [clairvoyant, clairaudiant, or psychic seer], or a necromancer [medium who consults the so-called spirits of the dead].

Invasion From Beyond

"For all that do these things are an abomination unto the Lord."

And while prophecy by psychic seers (wizards) is not specifically singled out in this text, verse 20 of the same chapter hands them a doomsday indictment:

"But the prophet, which shall presume to speak a word in my name, which I have not commanded him to speak, or that shall speak in the name of other gods, even that prophet shall surely die."

God simply condemns them to death — eternal death. In His eyes, to be a practitioner of occult phenomena is not just a violation of His standards; it is an open pledge of allegiance to His adversary, and as such cannot be tolerated.

How do the psychics react to that? I have told them these things — and it most definitely does not meet with much enthusiasm!

By the admission of the occultists and the authority of the Bible, we can speak of a clear-cut invasion by this God-condemned power, infiltrating the preconditioned minds of people at a time when responsible guidance has become a matter of utmost importance. There is firm historical evidence that when economic, political, and sociological confusion brings nations to a point of absolute moral devastation, people flock to the mystery cults, begging for answers to satisfy their guilt-ridden consciences. It happened in Babylon; it happened in Athens; it happened in the convulsive death-throes of the Roman Empire; and once more the same phenomenon is spreading today in the agonizing years of the 1970s. Modern man seeks out the occult in times of stress, but today there are no oracles to consult as in days past. Yet, with the overabundance of crystal balls, astrologers, palmists, mediums, psychics, seers, scientologists, clairvoyants, and devil worshipers, who needs them?[3] Christians certainly don't. But though God strictly forbids the old Chaldean practice of astrology, it has become one of the major tools of the psychic movement of the twentieth century, influencing millions of professed Christians in their daily activities.

The Soul Hustlers

What does it all signify or at least suggest?

It indicates that the time has come when supernatural forces are readying themselves for a conclusive battle for the mind and soul of mankind. Not wanting to be outmaneuvered by God, the Adversary's work is now entering a phase in which he is forcing all his power into his psychic prophets as communicators to reveal to the disillusioned world his supernatural ability as a major Cosmic Force. To show his diversified power, he tries to go beyond God, who for centuries used mainly prophets as His spokesmen. Satan is now pulling out all stops, attempting to force his will and power upon man through the various methods devised by the ancients, who, when under supernormal guidance, infiltrated the minds of nations with witchcraft and sorcery in its most primitive form.

Precisely how and when it will end no one knows, but the very fact that psychic interest is surging ahead without restraint seems to be indication enough that time is running out and that something is happening over which we have no control.

But what is *really* in the making for us, survivors of the space age? Why suddenly do 53 percent of Americans believe in occult phenomena? Why suddenly are there 2,350 horoscope computers, 1,200 daily astrology columns, satanic churches in every major city in the United States, psychics on every rostrum of the country's public auditoriums, and palmists along every interstate highway?

Psychics happily admit that their billion-dollar-a-year gross business is still growing at a fantastic rate and that they have no idea where or at what amount of profit it will end. They also proudly announce that their faith will become the main principle on which most mainline denominational churches will operate within the foreseeable future.

Most of those who unreservedly speak about this future fusion between spirit powers and the churches, and who make it so enticing, are not fully aware of the extent to which this has already taken place.

Invasion From Beyond

Arthur Ford, late medium and founder of the Spiritual Frontier Fellowship, speaking about the power of psychic phenomena, said in 1958,

"When we explore the psychic faculties we are not dabbling in something new and strange. We are just trying to remind the people in the churches of something that has always been part of the Christian Gospel, but has been neglected for centuries."[4] Never did he deny that a fusion of spiritualism and psychic doctrines and Christianity was his aim. Ford's group, however, was not the only organization responsible for the infiltration of psychic phenomena into the churches. Parapsychology — the study of psychic phenomena, also known as the "New Frontier" — is making inroads that are almost beyond belief. One of the recognized goals of this pseudoscience is to reconcile psychic phenomena with Christianity, each complementing the other.

Said Dr. Alson J. Smith, "Parapsychology . . . brings hope . . . for world peace, hope for more brotherly relations among men, hope for a new unity of religious faith."[5] "Doctrines, dogma, and form or organization all become secondary to the witness and power of the inner, supersensory life. Parapsychology will help unite Christendom by emphasizing that super-normal element that all denominations have in common, and minimizing those divisive elements that have their root in obsession."[6]

Another psychic advocate, Shaw Desmond, is convinced that soon the Christian religion will become the religion of the psychics. "Religion and science," he states bluntly, "will not only talk but will walk together."[7] When that happens, "the Atomic World will be riddled with the psychic, steered by the psychic."[8]

Can this be true? Is this what they have in mind? As a rule, they vehemently deny that Satan has anything to do with their missionary zeal.

"It's God who moves us," they claim. "What we are doing is holy and pure."

The Soul Hustlers

One of the greatest living psychic seers, Jeane Dixon, told me repeatedly while I was interviewing her for the biography, *My Life and Prophecies*, that "the same spirit that worked through Isaiah and John the Baptist also works through me." On many occasions she defended the old French astrologer Nostradamus's gift of prophecy by saying she was convinced he was indeed a man of God. Mrs. Dixon often commented that "if it were not for the prophetic gift God has given me, I would not be able to do what I am doing today." Yet she is not able to give a satisfactory explanation as to why God, having condemned clairvoyants and astrology in the Old Testament, would suddenly make an about-face and now allow His prophets to demonstrate these phenomena.

There are, however, some psychics who openly flaunt their devil connections and are proud of the fact that they have been singled out as a satanic tool.

One such man is Anton Szandor LaVey, the self-styled high priest of the First National Church of Satan in San Francisco. Eager to explain and justify his doctrines during a daylong interview, LaVey pointed out the obvious reasons for the existence of his church.

"I believe we are all Satanists," he said. "At least if not seven days a week, then perhaps one or two days a week. Yet Satan has never been fully understood. The devil in one form or another has always existed, but has never been able to stand up literally and speak for himself. His advocates have been practically nonexistent. This has now changed. Satan needs us as defenders if he is to come forth with an air of respectability.

"A true Satanist believes in God," he pointed out, "but as a force, a reckoning device, which balances the universe. God is a very powerful action-and-reaction device, but is not concerned whether people suffer pain or pleasure; whether they live or die; whether humans or animals are in misery, in torment, or in love. God is a force; Satan is the embodiment of all that we are concerned with on this earth."

26

He laughed.

"Through Satanism man's rightful place in nature is refound," he emphasized. "We are no longer suffocating weaklings groping in the dust, beseeching God to throw us a crumb of mercy. As sorcerers and sorceresses we are strong. We have only one sin — that is the sin of self-deceit."

For several hours we talked about his doctrines and the ways in which he is trying to spread his satanic beliefs. It was during this session that some of the more frightening aspects of this modern psychic church surfaced.

I asked LaVey about his views on prayer.

"Prayer is something I certainly don't believe in," the Satanist said, stretching out in his black chair, flanked by an ancient skull and an impressive collection of books on ritual magic. "Prayer is a nasty word. Prayer and hope represent apprehension, and apprehension represents not being sure of yourself, and of being without confidence in one's God. The true Satanist commands his God or simply states what he wants to have."

Thoughtfully he continued, "The sacrament of baptism too is important in Satanism. A person baptized in the name of Satan embraces the concept of Satanism for life, contrary to the idea of baptism being symbolic of cleansing a person from sin. The basic idea with us is that through baptism in the name of Satan, we invoke him to induce in the child all the appreciation for all the indulgences and gratifications of sin in that life so he will never make an attempt to stamp these things out.

"We dedicate our children to Satan."

Dangerous as this new church is to Christianity, its growth has not met with concerted opposition. Anton LaVey has his own explanation for this — one that may come critically close to the truth.

"The majority of church leaders I have been in contact with treat us with a rather amused acceptance," he smiled rather patronizingly. "I have not noticed any great controversy or reaction from religious sources, probably because their dogma and my dogma are basically very similar. The devil has been keeping them in business for so long that they can't afford to believe that he doesn't exist. They admit his existence, and my church gives them a shot in the arm. It backs their sermons with reality! They need us!"

The devil is out in the open — have no doubt about that — but his manifestations are not always so decidedly anti-Christian. Many of them are cloaked in a disguise of godliness and difficult to identify.

Most people like to turn their backs on this infiltration of devil-phenomena. What they prefer to erase from their minds is the realization that God has never changed His criteria; He is unchanging, and something condemned as ungodly remains condemned forever.

Throughout the Bible there are many specific tests that must be fulfilled by those who claim to be true prophets of God. Inasmuch as this claim is extensively used by today's psychics, we are justified in using the Bible in judgment on them. Prophetic phenomena are the greatest single exhibit of supernatural power among the psychics. They prophesy through clairvoyance, clairaudience, crystal balls, spirit possession, witchcraft, and astrology: varied methods, but all reaching for the same goal of foretelling future events. Working with these prophets of today enables one to obtain a rare insight into the operations and beliefs of these people. They are undeniably a breed all by themselves, surrounded by admirers, greatly sought after as public speakers, and highly revered for their uncanny ability to peek beyond the threshhold of the unknown; however, when their life style and works are compared with the biblical requirements for true prophets, something happens.

Inasmuch as the word *prophet* means "someone who speaks for God," God has always zealously guarded this assignment. An ambassador cannot be regarded as such unless recognized by his government, and the same relationship exists between God and His true prophets. It is most revealing to see how fast a psychic prophet loses his luster when these tests are applied.

As a prophetic guidebook, the Bible contains not only world-shattering prophecies, but also ways in which similarly guided prophecies can be recognized. Listing *all* the tests of true prophets and applying them to psychic prophets would certainly reach beyond the scope of this book, but there are at least eight which we can apply to the occult practitioners. Upon examining the results, their shortcomings are quickly exposed, for the uncompromising tests are very specific.

1. A true prophet does not lie (Jer. 28:9).

Of all the prophetic requirements, this one assuredly ranks among the most important. It clearly states that God's prophets are always right and that in their work as spokesmen for God, there is simply no margin for error. God does not make mistakes. There must be 100 percent fulfillment, and it is at this point that we begin to wonder about today's prophets. They allege to be true prophets — yet their failures are many. How do they explain them?

Sometime ago in a lengthy discussion with Dr. Regis Riesenman, a well-known psychologist and parapsychologist in Arlington, Virginia, this subject arose, and Dr. Riesenman made some remarkably frank statements.

"I have studied psychics and prophets for more than fifty years," he stated matter-of-factly, "and have found less than twenty with an accuracy of 80-85 percent at the most. No psychic ever goes beyond that point." Other researchers support this conclusion, which indicates that in their predictive work, today's prophets have a percentage of failures that makes their claims highly questionable. Even the greatest of the modern prophets must acknowledge defeat when confronted with Jeremiah 28:9. In all my discussions with psychics regarding this point, one thing is apparent: since most of them credit "vibrations" emanating from a person as the channel through which they receive their information, they also blame this same transmission medium for their failures.

"I was not tuned in on his vibrations when he changed his plans," they invariably tell me. "My initial prediction was a true prophecy, but I wasn't informed of the change in plans. . . ." A poor excuse, yet one widely accepted by both psychics and followers.

2. A true prophet prophesies in the name of the Lord (2 Peter 1:21).

Although it is vitally important for a "spokesman" to speak in the name of those who sent him, this test does not concern psychics in the least.

Then how do they predict?

Experience has shown me that they seldom permit God to enter into their work. One is most likely to hear "I predict" or "I forecast" or "I foresee. . . . " No psychic ever does (or dares to!) make predictions in the name of the Lord; he simply does not speak for God — and deep down he knows it!

But there are more tests facing the prophets of today.

3. A true prophet does not give his own private interpretation of prophecy (2 Peter 1:20).

In this instance, too, they fail. I have listened to psychics give interpretations of biblical prophecy, only to change them again when trying to make the prophecy fit a different audience. This they do, not only with biblical prophecy, but with their own predictions as well, depending upon the impression they wish to impart.

An example of a psychic's interpretating of prophecy concerns Jeane Dixon and her now-famous vision of the serpent that slithered in bed with her after having entered her bedroom through the closed window on Nineteenth Street in Washington, D.C.

Startled, Mrs. Dixon rose on her side and stared at the serpent. What was it? What did it signify?

Jeane told me the meaning when I interviewed her for one of my books a few years later. Letting her mind drift back to that memorable vision, she said softly,

"It was Christ appearing to me in the form of a serpent, promising me all the wisdom of the ages if I'd only follow him. The steady gaze of the reptile was permeated with love, goodness, strength, and knowledge."

To Mrs. Dixon, it was a highlight in prophecy, for she claimed that after staring into the serpent's eyes, she received the solemn assurance that all would be well if she'd only follow his advice! But was it Christ?

Not wanting to accept her interpretation of that vision, I probed deeper because of the identity with the biblical account of the serpent in the Garden of Eden. After discussing this with her, emphasizing the similarity, Mrs. Dixon suddenly made a 180-degree turn.

"Come to think of it," she interrupted rather hurriedly, "it really didn't touch me. I wasn't defiled by it! Now I remember. It really wasn't Christ who promised me all that wisdom. . . . *It was the Devil masquerading as a serpent. He tried to entice me. . . .*"

In later years, this switch in prophetic interpretation caused the disillusionment of many of her followers, and they wondered about the source of Mrs. Dixon's inspiration. This sudden change and her own private brand of Bible interpretation has placed her in clear violation of this all-important test. She fits the psychics' pattern.

4. A true prophet points out the sins and transgressions of the people against God (Isa. 58:1).

Have you ever heard a "prophet" do this? Today's psychics depend heavily on the financial rewards of their "gift," and there is only one way a modern prognosticator can keep his following: by forecasting those bits of enlightenment needed for the temporary emotional satisfaction of their clients. Telling customers that they are sinning against God certainly does not promote popularity — and popularity and recommendations is what the psychic business is all about.

5. A true prophet is to warn the people of God's coming judgment (Isa. 24:20,21; Rev. 14:6,7).

This falls under the same basic category as the previous test. While this "warning of the people against God's judgment" is one of the main functions of a godly prophet, this prerequisite cannot be found among the phenomena we encounter today.

6. A true prophet can be recognized by the results of his work (Matt. 7:17-20).

All biblical prophecies deal with the uplifting of the human soul to God. It was never God's intention for evil to befall His people. His predictions relayed through His prophets, *when dealing with the welfare or punishment of His people,* were invariably conditional. Repentance was always the condition, and often God postponed or completely canceled His planned chastisement because His people turned away from evil.

Is this what is happening today? I recall some dire predictions made by leading psychics, informing us of the imminent assassinations of President Kennedy, Robert F. Kennedy, Mahatma Gandhi, Martin Luther King, Dag Hammarskjold, and others. I recall predictions of airplane crashes, earthquakes, fiery disasters, and railroad tragedies — *but the strange, unexplainable fact is that these warnings were never issued to the potential victims.* God *always* warned those who were to be involved; the psychics do not. Research indicates that the above-mentioned occurrences were indeed predicted beforehand (hourlong interviews with reliable informants testify to that), but the *victims* somehow were never given a chance. It was not a matter of God's punishment being called into action, for assassinations never bring anyone close to God. It was the result of the action by *another* power who played his hand mercilessly.

God reaches beyond the assassination of statesmen; the outcome of a horse race; the fluctuation of the stockmarket; or the future marriages of a beauty queen. Indeed, a *true* prophet can be recognized by the fruits of his work. It is clearly evident that the result of the work of today's prophets is not the work of God.

7. A true prophet recognizes the incarnation of Christ (1 John 4:1-3).

This simply means that a real prophet acknowledges Christ as the Son of God. Jesus cannot be considered a reincarnation of someone else, nor can He be regarded as a superpsychic human being.

Since the majority of today's occultists are not to be found among the theologians, the violations of this test are not always easily discernible. Psychics express varied views of Christ. The famous psychic Edgar Cayce, now deceased, presented a profusion of material which he and his followers claim proves the theory of reincarnation. His books all advocate this Eastern non-Christian philosophy, yet nonbiblical as it may be, his "insights" are accepted by millions of churchgoers the world over.

Early in my psychic research, I began to compare Edgar Cayce, the Master Psychic, to the biblical tests. Though he transgresses every one of them in different degrees, the test requiring a true prophet to recognize and admit the incarnation of Christ is one he violates most strongly.

Cayce had a unique style of receiving and relaying his prophetic impulses. Known as "readings," the abundance of supernaturally supplied information was given by him after submitting to a deep state of relaxation, ending in a trance. When someone would then request data on a specific subject, the mouth of the unconscious psychic would commence to furnish the desired information.

Cayce failed, however, when it came to recognizing the divinity of Christ, even though he claimed that it was Christ personally who gave him his power to prophesy.

This incriminating violation took place when his Inspiration attempted to reveal to Cayce's questioner detailed information regarding the life of Christ. Whatever we know concerning the life of Christ is rather sketchy — though true — because the Bible does not speak of His life in the period from his twelfth through his thirtieth years. The prophetic power operating Edgar Cayce, however, professed to know *all* the details of those hidden years and was more than anxious to fill this void.

Excited, the questioner began to ask for answers, probing into the unknown mysteries of the life of Christ. A recent book, *Edgar Cayce's Story of Jesus*,[9] tells it all; whereas it was written under the pretext that Cayce's responses were God-inspired, the very first paragraph of the first chapter reveals the actual nature of the power operating Edgar Cayce.

"When did Jesus become aware that he would be the Saviour of the world?" the inquirer asked for "reading" 2067-7.

There was a deep sigh. Then the words flowed from the mouth of the unconscious psychic.

When He fell in Eden.

"Does this mean that Jesus had been Adam?" he continued his questioning.

Cayce answered, *Know this is the soul-entity* [Joshua] . . . *the same soul-entity was their first-born Joseph . . . as Zend* [father of Zoroaster] . . . *as the same entity as Enoch. . . .*

He denied the divinity of Christ! By alleging that Christ was merely a reincarnation of Adam, Joseph, Zend, and many others, he pulled Him down to the level of a lowly human being, thereby violating one of the most sacred tests of a true prophet.

8. A true prophet's words will be in harmony with those of prophets who have preceded him (Isa. 8:20).

In discussing the relative merits of the psychic prophets and their various claims, I have often encountered hard criticism from both the psychics and their followers, for psychics emphatically believe and promote the idea that they are God's own prophets.

One such confrontation occurred not long ago on a midnight talk show on a network-affiliated radio station in San Francisco. I had been on the air several hours condemning today's psychics and mediums on the basis of the biblical tests, when suddenly it happened.

The emcee and I had just discussed test number eight, which states that a true prophet's words must be in harmony with those of the prophets who have preceded him, when a barrage of little red phone lights illuminated the switchboard in front of us. It was an audience-participation show, where reaction from the listeners is encouraged, and this point had really hit home.

I picked up the phone and pressed the first red button.

The lady on the other end immediately voiced her disapproval of my statement determinedly.

"Jeane Dixon *does* meet that qualification," she said vehemently. "She *is* a true prophet of God, no matter what you say. She said so herself on television last night."

For a moment the emcee and I looked at each other. Bemused, he shrugged his shoulders; I reacted vocally.

"What did she use to prove her claim?" I asked quietly, wondering what it could be this time.

"Mrs. Dixon said that she had predicted the 'Watergate' scandal," the lady countered, "and that the Holy Bible had also predicted 'Watergate' — so that shows she meets the requirements of test number eight."

Stunned silence. There are moments when words fail — this was one of them. I thought I knew the psychics, but this was a new one.

"On what does she base this?" I queried. By this time I couldn't help but smile at this ludicrous claim. The emcee flashed me a grin of encouragement.

"Nehemiah 8:1 was her test," the voice answered. "It says there that Ezra met with the people in front of the water gate. And since she has also predicted 'Watergate,' this proves that she is indeed a prophet of God!"

Hilarious? No, sad. If today's "prophets" have to resort to misrepresenting the words of the power they claim to serve, then they most assuredly cannot be on the side of God. I have often wondered why psychics who have a publicized accuracy of 100 percent in predicting assassinations and violent deaths can dare to boast that God is behind them. This is not the way God operates.

Several surveys have been conducted since the Second

World War for the purpose of ascertaining exactly what this nation believes. The latest Roper Organization survey,[10] showing that 53 percent of the population have faith in psychic phenomena, is the most precise in this field and the most damaging to our reputation as a "Christian nation." Many of the country's leading parapsychologists have conducted exhaustive studies on scores of psychics with high PAQs (Prophetic Accuracy Quotient), and although the outcomes are always interesting, they have never reached conclusive results.

This may be changing, however, thanks to the CIA.

It all began when four former U.S. spies — two from the CIA and two others from U.S. Army Intelligence — decided to embark on a project that would enable them to evaluate electronically the conscious and subconscious sincerity of the human voice in order to determine the honesty of the answers supplied by the informant.

Experienced in electronic gadgetry, they focused their attention on the microtremor found in the human voice box. What surfaced after considerable experimentation is now called the Psychological Stress Evaluator, commonly known as the PSE.

What is it? How does it work? And more important, is it reliable?

It is known that the human voice does not merely consist of audible frequencies — the *sound* we hear — but also contains an *inaudible* frequency, called a microtremor. All living beings, animals and humans, have this microtremor within them. With humans, it is tremor between eight and twelve beats (vibrations) per second.

We are unable to detect these tremors, but the PSE can! The quality of the human voice is susceptible to the amount of stress one may be under while speaking or answering specific questions. To the human ear, the answers may sound perfectly normal and honest, free of "guilt-revealing" sound variations. But the PSE senses the difference and can record the changes in the inaudible FM microtremor frequency on a strip of electrocardiograph paper.

The more severe the lie, the higher the tension is in the human body, which results in a suppression of the micro-tremors in the voice box. We are unable to hear or measure this stress, but the PSE can; when it does, the stress reveals itself on the chart as a conscious or subconscious attempt to deceive.

In its reaction to these tremor fluctuations, the PSE is extremely accurate. Says criminologist Mike Kradz of Dektor (manufacturers of the instrument), "A series of tests was performed with the PSE to test its validity and accuracy. Tested on 'To Tell The Truth,' it scored a success of 94.7 percent! In another test series, in conjunction with tradi-tional lie-detection tests, it scored an impressive 91 percent. When used on twenty-six criminal cases, it resulted in cor-roborating the results of the traditional lie-detector for a full 100 percent."

While the *Psychological Stress Evaluator* searches for signs of deception by dissecting the vibrations in the human voice, the *polygraph* does this by simultaneously measuring and recording various bodily functions such as heartbeat, blood pressure, and respiration rate. Because voice vibra-tions and microtremors *and* heartbeat, blood pressure, and respiration rate tend to be affected when a person attempts to lie or deceive, both the PSE and the polygraph are used widely in criminal investigation.

Criminologists, psychologists, investigators, and others who have tested and used the PSE endorse Mike Kradz's conclusion wholeheartedly.

Dr. James W. Worth, psychologist at Washington and Lee University, Lexington, Virginia, states, "The PSE is neither an occult phenomenon nor a huckster's trick, but a technological breakthrough."

Lt. Ray Aldrich of the Baldwin Park (California) Police Department agrees: "PSE is an extremely significant de-velopment in criminal investigation," he says. "It's a valu-able tool in clearing innocent suspects. We can tell quickly if a

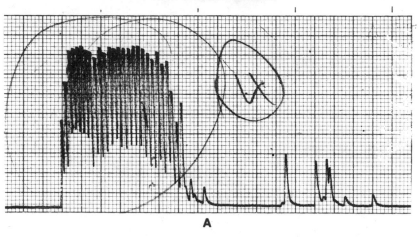

A

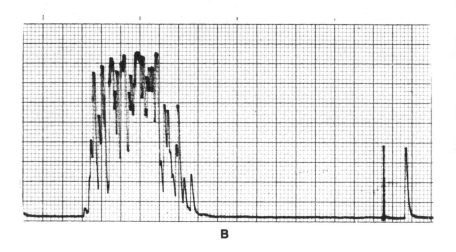

B

Figure 1. The PSE graphs shown above are typical examples of an answer *with stress* (A), and one *without stress* (B). The top graph shows severe emotional stress, unually associated with a conscious attempt to deceive. The one below is relatively stressless, and can be considered indicative of an honest reaction. Both these graphs are located somewhere on the outer perimeter of possible PSE reactions. Answers given in reply to questions usually display reactions somewhere in between these two.

person is telling the truth." (See figure 1.) It is no wonder that the CIA, FBI, Army Intelligence, and approximately 171 law enforcement agencies in the United States are now using the PSE to check on their suspects. Foreign governments also are beginning to rely on this new development, for King Hussein's intelligence experts trained side by side with those from Israel at Dektor's PSE training facility.

Interesting to note is that several independent PSE operators used the instrument for some of the most intriguing controversies of the last few years. In analyzing the voice of John Dean as he related his version of the Watergate cover-up, it gave him an awesome 90-plus percent for honesty. More recently, one of the inventors of the PSE used it on the tape-recorded interviews in connection with the now-famous Chappaquiddick case involving U.S. Sen. Ted Kennedy. Basing his conclusion on the examination of more than a thousand feet of tape recordings made of Senator Kennedy's version of the incident, Col. Charles R. McQuiston states unequivocally that "I am thoroughly convinced Kennedy told the truth about Chappaquiddick. There is no doubt about it." Without wanting to dig into this still-smoldering controversy, we must keep in mind that this conclusion was based only on the information available. The question remains, was it all told?

The PSE is indeed a terrifying weapon in the fight against untruth. It shows that man was not "programmed" to lie and that lying is contrary to human nature. No matter how well we may attempt to conceal our true feelings and knowledge, the subconscious *knows* and will reveal the truth once the key to its knowledge is inserted.

The PSE, I believe, is the key.

Careful evaluation of PSE charts has shown that it probes even deeper than was at first anticipated. Series of test cases I have conducted with the PSE have convinced me that the instrument not only can provide telltale clues to conscious or subconscious attempts to deceive, but can also reveal *convictions* or the *lack* thereof.

One test series was of particular interest to me. Having

used the PSE on criminal cases and as a guide to vocational interest for college students, I often stumbled upon a guilt-complex in asking, in a course-comparison test at a religious college: "Do you live up to the Ten Commandments to the best of your ability?" The answer was always "yes"; the PSE reaction was invariably negative, the stress indicating either insincerity or deception.

From this emerged an idea to formulate a "Ten Commandments" test, using all ten of them in one test separated by the necessary control and irrelevant questions.

After trying it out on a college student with surprising results — surprising to him, that is — I conducted the same PSE test on an eleven-year-old. Instructing her to answer "no" to all my questions, I recorded the Ten Commandments interview. (The PSE uses only recorded voices, not live sounds.) The reason for stipulating negative answers is that if she were lying when answering "no," the PSE would find her out.

Following my instructions, she denied violating any. Then the sound was fed into the PSE, and within a mere fifteen minutes the results were available. It charged her with failing to observe the fourth, fifth, eighth, ninth, and tenth commandments. *The reactions were in different degrees, but there was a revealing guilt factor for each one of them!*

By now you are wondering what possible relationship there can be between the PSE and the psychics and mediums, the astrologers and the crystal-gazers.

The tracings on my charts signify to me that it is the only known weapon that can furnish us with extremely accurate indications as to the honesty and sincerity of the psychics. Tested on the PSE, they cannot hide their insecurity, their doubts, and — more important — their violations of true biblical norms. Do they *really* believe they fulfill the tests of the true prophets? The PSE can take their answers apart and show their sincerity or lack of it. Are they consciously planning to bring institutional Christianity to the brink of spiritual chaos by saturating it with psychic phenomena? Do they *really* believe in the raging spiritual battle between Christ and Satan? Will there actually be a second coming of Christ? Do they honestly believe that God is the source of their prophetic power?

The Psychological Stress Evaluator can check their revelations for truth or deception. If God's enemy is indeed their guiding force, then their audible answers should be fair game for the discriminating power of the PSE.

This book is the result of an in-depth study of practitioners of supernatural phenomena, based on their reactions to a list of eighty-seven questions. Their answers, fed into a computer for tabulation, have resulted in a precise account of their major beliefs and convictions. In order to determine the true, unvarnished aims of this movement that is attempting to gain a stranglehold on Christianity, we have fed the accumulated oral answers into the electronic circuitry of the Psychic Stress Evaluator. The PSE has withstood the test; it has revealed what the devil-inspired thrust is trying to conceal. It has exposed their true doctrines and intentions — something of which every Christian should be aware.

The devil has never been able to capture *completely* the God-instilled subconscious mind. This inability can now be used against him and his promoters.

In evaluating the answers of the country's leading occultists, I have not worked from preconceived notions. I do not attempt to accuse them of either outright dishonesty or outright deception. There is always the possibility that they themselves are deceived, but subconsciously they *know* the difference between fact and fiction.

The tabulation of the admitted claims and doctrines of the psychics is the result of the genius of the computer. The evaluation of their secret convictions or plans come to us through the unbiased graphs of the PSE.

It's "Big Brother" watching us all over again . . . but this time for the sake of honesty.

The PSE speaks where we can't.

The Soul Hustlers

Notes

[1]*National Enquirer*, 18 March 1975.

[2]Rene Noorbergen, *Jeane Dixon – My Life and Prophecies* (New York: William Morrow & Co., 1969), p. 153.

[3]A "psychic prophet" or "psychic seer" is someone able to forecast events on the basis of supernatural information received from an ungodly source. The general term *psychics*, on the other hand, refers to all those who profess to base their phenomena on psychic powers — powers lying outside the sphere of physical science or knowledge — whether or not they include prophecy.

[4]*Spiritual Frontiers*, Vol. 3, No. 3 (May-June 1958):2.

[5]Alson J. Smith, *Religion and the New Psychology* (1951), p. 151.

[6]Ibid., p. 174.

[7]*Psychic Pitfalls* (London: n.p., 1954), pp. 269-70.

[8]Ibid.

[9]Edited by Jeffrey Furst (New York: Berkley Publishing, 1970).

[10]This survey was conducted according to professional standards among all strata of the population, not specifically among readers of psychic publications. The Roper Organization describes this poll as representative of the total American population.

Checking Satan's Realm

2

2   Checking Satan's Realm

2 IT WAS ANTON SZANDOR LA VEY, HIGH PRIEST of the First National Church of Satan who said, "The Devil is ruling this world. All I am doing is giving homage where homage is due."

It came at the end of a daylong interview, but it might have been one of the most important statements he ever made. If this is really true — if Satan is indeed ruling this tired old globe of ours — then now is the time to investigate thoroughly the extent of his realm and seriously attempt to establish its spiritual boundaries, both inward and on the outer perimeter.

The borders of his mental penetration can be outlined by measuring the degree to which his supernatural manifestations have gained a foothold in the life of the average American; the outer limits of Satan's realm can be estimated by establishing a meaningful figure showing the number of people whose allegiance is clearly on his side by both action and missionary zeal.

The Soul Hustlers

I have been on the investigative side of psychic phenomena for many years, and with each new book I uncover new angles. Scanning my collection of books and checking my files dealing with the subject, it is obvious to me that thus far the scientific investigation of psychic phenomena has been rather one-sided. It has always focused on the premise that psychic phenomena are natural phenomena devoid of any supernatural influence. To the investigators, any suggestion that there might be a supernatural power pulling the strings, working behind the scenes, is admitting that the phenomena work on principles that are un-human and impossible to explain. Denying the role of a supernatural power in psychic affairs, they probe the various manifestations, trusting to discover a natural explanation enabling them to duplicate the phenomena at will by orthodox scientific methods.

Thus far their search has been in vain. Perhaps the psychics themselves are partially to blame for this failure. Parapsychologists are reluctant to admit that their subjects have a rather confused outlook on what they practice and that as a result their basic experiences are colored by their degree of disbelief. Most psychics have a somewhat limited faith in the Bible, accepting only what their psychic sense tells them is reliable. Professing to believe in the Bible, they nevertheless shun all areas that tend to disclaim their supernatural ability, interpreting other passages in the light of their private visions. Yet, with all these mental reservations, they still claim that their specific "gift" is undoubtedly the equivalent of a certain biblical gift (usually prophecy), and thus their counsel should be heeded, for the Bible is infallible.

Parapsychology — the study of psychic phenomena in its broadest sense — has never been widely recognized as a legitimate science. It is always difficult to build a science on something intangible — especially if this "something intangible" is expressed in many different ways by the thousands of pseudoscientists involved.

Regardless of all the problems facing parapsychological

research, experimentation in supernormal affairs in the last few decades has been breaking out of its earlier, self-imposed limitations. The aforementioned Roper survey, commissioned by the weekly *National Enquirer*, more than confirms the extent of this dramatic change. This survey is the first scientifically conducted and comprehensive survey of American attitudes toward psychic phenomena, the result of personal interviews with two thousand individuals.

What does it reveal?

The figures are harsh and frightening. They indicate that a staggering 66 percent of all white-collar workers believe in psychic phenomena.

The results of how people reacted to the question "Do you believe in psychic phenomena or not?" are shown in table 1.

The *National Enquirer* prints more psychic-oriented material than any other publication in the United States and was of course interested in the outcome of this survey, as it has a direct bearing on their circulation. I doubt very much, however, whether its leadership envisioned this kind of a reaction.

The survey contains some disturbing facts:

1. *Of those in the age bracket of 18-29 – that segment of the United States population highly influential in forming future policy as well as possessing the decisive vote in the country's major political elections – a full 65 percent believe in psychic phenomena*. Youthful enthusiasm, growing dissatisfaction with the times, and a waxing belief in the "evolution of the mind" are all contributing factors to this dramatic condition. In older age levels, *faith in the occult powers diminishes to 32 percent at age 60*. Unfortunately the poll measured only current attitudes, and this does not tell us whether the heady confidence of youth will evolve into a similar diminution of belief as the generation grows older.

2. *More women than men believe in the power of psychic phenomena* with the percentages being 56 versus 48. This may be indicative of a mounting danger, propelling us to an even

47

TABLE 1

	Believe in	Don't Believe	Don't Know
Total	53	37	10
Sex			
Male	48	40	12
Female	56	34	10
Age			
18–29	65	27	8
30–44	57	33	10
45–59	51	39	10
60 and over	32	53	15
Income			
Under $6,000	36	48	16
$6,000–$12,000	54	36	10
$12,000–$18,000	57	34	9
$18,000 and over	59	32	9
Race			
White	54	37	9
Black	34	36	30
Geographic Area			
Northeast	54	37	9
Midwest	53	38	9
South	44	42	14
West	66	26	8
Education			
College	68	25	7
High School	52	38	10
Grade School	26	55	19
Occupation			
Executive/Professional	55	33	12
White Collar	66	27	7
Blue Collar	50	37	13

higher total acceptance of psychic phenomena in the future. Women raise most of our children, select their early reading material, guide their faith, and help formulate their values. This in combination with their own developing desires have resulted in 65 percent of eighteen-year-olds believing in the Faith of the Age of Aquarius.

3. *The more affluent, the higher the percentage of faith in*

the occult. The survey shows that at the poverty level of $6,000, only 36 of every 100 individuals find it emotionally satisfying to believe in psychic phenomena; theirs is a fight for daily survival, leaving little time for superstition. But when the paycheck reaches $18,000 or more, leisure time becomes more prevalent and the fascination of the supernatural changes into belief. At the present time, it is "mod" to accept its phenomena, and as a result 59 percent of those in that bracket ascribe credibility to the occult.

4. *Education is closely related to the degree of acceptance.* Among people with a college education, an alarming 68 percent of those interviewed freely admit to a belief in psychic powers. A grade-school education generates 26 believers per 100; a high-school education guarantees 52 out of 100. Is it possible that the high-school and college courses in psychic phenomena now being taught throughout the country are beginning to pay off for the psychic industry?

Not long ago, the majority of schools frowned on the very idea of teaching parapsychological courses; now an opposite trend is evident. As yet, there are no doctorates available in parapsychology, but a Ph.D in sociology or psychology and an additional year or two as apprentice to an established researcher in parapsychology are enough to qualify one as a parapsychologist. Those already practicing their profession are literally deluged with letters from high-school teachers begging for instruction.

As a direct outgrowth of the subsequent training, high schools and colleges now offer courses in ESP (extrasensory perception), psychokinesis, clairvoyance, precognition, psychometry, dream interpretation, telepathy, psychic photography, astral projection, materialization and dematerialization, as well as other mysterious facets of the psychic world. This is all transpiring as predicted by some of the country's major psychics. Referring to one of these phenomena, David N. Bubar, well-known psychic minister from Memphis, Tennessee, told me that "the practice of what has been called man's energy force leaving his body during sleep will be accepted as most common around the end of this century. It is an occult practice that was used in ancient days, and owing to the tremendous emphasis placed on psychic phenomena, it will be revived.

"Man will again harness this power," he claims, "to the extent that he will be able to keep his physical body in a perfect state of existence with all its functions operating normally, while his intellect journeys off to faraway places, collecting information or conducting business. After completion, I see the energy force return to the body and inhabit it once again, retaining all information collected on its astral trip.

"Psychic learning will be the trend of the future," he concludes.

A recent experience by the noted Israeli psychic, Uri Geller, has demonstrated an ability that parapsychologists claim is precisely what Bubar refers to — astral projection. After several unexplainable happenings involving disappearances and appearances in foreign places, Uri admits he's had enough. There will be no more astral projection or out-of-the-body experiences for him — at least that is what he says. "I'm not going to do it," Geller told the reporter of the *National Tattler*. "I have done it only four times. And twice it seemed to be more of a dream. Another time, there was a mix-up. But once my spirit left my body and went to Brazil.

"I was really scared because the first thing that hit me was, how do I get back? I didn't have a passport or money. A man pulled out his wallet and gave me money.

"And, of course," Uri continued, "my body was with Dr. Puharich back in New York. Suddenly Brazilian currency appeared in my hand.

"It was an incredible experience. But scary."[1]

It is no wonder that educators are extremely interested in psychic phenomena, for developing this ability would indeed create a total upheaval of our educational process.

5. *The survey deals a blow to a favorite "white" belief* — the erroneous idea that blacks are more superstitious than

whites. With the same education, same income, and same social standing, 34 percent of blacks and a powerful 54 percent of whites believe in psychic phenomena. It may come as a surprise to many, *but this survey does prove that the white race in the United States leans more to a faith in the occult than does the black!*

6. *Is there perhaps a geographical area in the United States where the occult has not gained a solid foothold?* Roper has done a highly commendable job in setting its teams to work probing the minds of two thousand people. When we compare the distribution of psychic believers among the four major geographic areas of the country, the results are both alarming and reassuring.

The South, home of the Bible Belt and conservative Christianity, is a full 9 percentage points behind the Midwest in psychic belief (44 percent in the South), 10 points behind the Northeast, and a striking 12 points behind the Far West! The South is the only region in the country where psychic followers are not in the majority! But 44 out of every 100 Southerners is still a threatening percentage.

Causing more concern was a survey conducted in 1975 which revealed that *today only 40 of every 100 Americans attend church regularly.* Dr. Sterling Cary, president of the New York-based National Council of Churches, however, was not at all disillusioned by this.

"A lot of people who don't go to church are acting out their faith in other arenas — politics, unions, civil rights organizations, and education," Cary rationalized. "If we include these people, the percentage would be much larger than 40 percent."[2] But these people do *not* attend church. A union hall, a civil rights meeting, or a political rally is *not* the same as a place where God is worshiped; consequently we cannot include their number to increase the percentage of church attendance. *Realistically speaking, only 40 percent of Americans attend church somewhat regularly, 29 percent go occasionally, 6 percent attend on holidays only, and 24 percent never set foot in a church!* No figures have been compiled as to where the psychic believers who constitute 53 percent of the population fit in; but it can be assumed that some have crossed over into the group of church-going Americans. A possible conclusion that emerges from these statistics is that a large section of those who attend church regularly are in actuality pledging allegiance to both God and His adversary. Suddenly the figure of 117 million psychic believers — that 53 percent — takes on an even more ominous appearance.

What is so appealing about supernormal manifestations that the uncommitted as well as professing Christians turn to these mystery cults? Psychics readily suggest that their faith is more "up-to-date" and that their methods were used by Christ while He was on the earth. In fact, *The Spiritualist Manual*, 1955 edition, makes the allegation that the Bible is nothing more than a compilation of spiritualist (psychic) phenomena. The opening of the iron gate for Peter by an angel (Acts 12:7-10) is an example. So also are "clairvoyant appearances" (as of Moses and Elijah on the Mount and of Christ after the resurrection); speaking in unknown tongues (as at Pentecost); trances (as of Paul, 2 Cor. 12:2,4); "direct spirit writing" (as on the palace walls of Babylon, Dan. 5:5); "levitation" (as when Philip was caught away, Acts 8:39,40); "clairvoyance and clairaudience" (as with the voice heard by Saul the persecutor, Acts 9:4,7); healing (as by Jesus, Peter, and Paul); and dreams and visions (as with John the Revelator and Daniel). These are all considered to have been psychic phenomena and the results of the workings of the spirit world. All the miracles wrought by Jesus while on earth are considered by spiritualists to be psychic phenomena.

"Ours is a more exalted type of religion," I have been told repeatedly. "Ours is a religion of the future. We are on the way to give humanity the same powers that Christ had."

One of the predominant figures in the formative years of the psychic movement was the creator of the Sherlock Holmes novels, Sir Arthur Conan Doyle. He once commented, "The ultimate merit of that revelation which came in so humble a shape, will be the simplification of religion, the breaking down of the barriers between the sects, and a universal creed which will combine the ethics of real Christianity with direct spiritual communication."[3] "Spiritualism will sweep the world, and make it a better place to live. When it rules over all the world, it will banish the blood of Christ. Spiritualism has a mighty mission to fulfill."[4]

It is precisely these goals and claims that bring in the converts. Having written several psychic biographies in the course of my work as a journalist, I have become well-acquainted with some of the country's great psychics. The interesting twist is that even though they speak of fame, intense excitement, and the spiritual fulfillment that their profession supplies, the truth is that they are still among the most insecure people in the world. They have exchanged the values of Christianity for a reliance on unstable principles of dubious quality.

So they don't believe what we do — but what *do* they believe? With whom do we Christians coexist in our society?

Probing Satan's realm can be accomplished in various ways, depending upon which facet of it is under investigation. Although parapsychology claims to explore the psychic world, incredible as it seems, the *spiritual* aims of the psychics have never been the target of a conscientious probe. Hans Holzer, parapsychologist and research director of the New York Committee for the Investigation of Paranormal Occurrences, claims that there are definite limits to psychic investigations.

"There are only *three* ways by which one can investigate the various phases of the occult field," Holzer writes. "The first, and most difficult still, is the purely scientific approach, relying as it does on outmoded tools and concepts. The second road is what I like to call the parascientific road, including the metaphysical, which explores the realms of the occult by orderly means, albeit by standards more attuned to the realities of the occult world. Finally, there is the third approach, "personal and individual experience which cannot be communicated to others in precisely the same terms as it occurs to the individual concerned, but which nevertheless is a valid experience leading to some form of illumination."[5]

What Holzer disregards is the religious aspects of psychic phenomena. By completely ignoring the existence of the two opposing powers, God and Satan, that compete for supremacy in the minds and lives of men, he is brushing aside the controversy that once rocked the universe (Isa. 14: 12-14).

There is another way of researching the psychic phenomena that now have 117 million Americans in their grasp. We can check their doctrines and compare them with Christian beliefs. We can examine their aims, expose their methods of operation to accepted Christian values, and measure the magnitude of the danger facing Christianity.

What *do* they believe?

Do they meet the biblical tests of true prophets?

Does a *true* prophet relay God's warnings by the use of astrology, psychic vibrations, or a crystal ball?

Does God allow His prophets to deny the deity of Christ?

There are literally hundreds of related questions that require well-defined answers, and usual methods of scientific testing of psychic occurrences do not provide them. Of the hundreds of psychic seers who operate within the geographical boundaries of the United States, only a relatively few attain a percentage of accuracy that exceeds mere chance — yet most of them claim to have a God-given ability to prophecy. It is usually with a great deal of pride that the country's leading psychic prophets point to their fulfilled predictions.

"During the course of my lectures and of the question-and-answer periods, I have often noticed that my audience is somewhat shocked when I mention that I am sometimes wrong in my predictions," says Daniel Logan, spiritualist psychic from New York City.

"No one seems to expect a doctor, or an architect, or an engineer or a carpenter to be infallible; but the poor medium apparently is required to be completely on target at all times.

Unfortunately the psychic medium is only a human being dealing with human situations; the flesh is weak, and the situations are variable. To me, it seems that if the psychic gives evidence of a reasonable percentage of accuracy then he has done something quite extraordinary. Given the circumstances in which a psychic works and the material with which he deals, it seems to me remarkable that I am able to maintain an accuracy of eighty percent."

But then he complains, *"The attitude of the public is not that I am right eighty percent of the time, but that I am wrong twenty percent of the time."* [6]

No matter how he defends his gift, his inspiration does fail him at least 20 percent of the time. Jeane Dixon, the woman who launched America on its mid-twentieth-century course of psychic prophecy, also has her failures. Reputed to have reached accuracies of up to 85 percent, those who know her intimately and are cognizant of her tremendous number of unfulfilled predictions do not credit her with more than a 16 percent PAQ today. Perhaps the aging process must be taken into consideration.

Peter Hurkos, the Dutch-American psychic who has often doubled as investigator for law enforcement agencies, has a PAQ of approximately 80 percent. Ingel Swan, Harold Sherman, M. D. Dijkshoorn, Olaf Johnsson, Penny South, Robert Strong, Robert Nelson, Edward Snedeker, and many others in the psychic field also have varying low rates of prophetic fulfillment. Although their excuses for their shortcomings may vary, all without exception lack total accuracy.

Diverse as these psychic prophets may be when it comes to fulfillment, they do agree on one point and that is their abhorrence of being tested by someone regarded as an expert in the field of parapsychology.

They simply have no faith in parapsychologists.

"How can a parapsychologist who is not a psychic devise a way to test a psychic?" they invariably ask. "The very fact that he is devoid of psychic ability proves his ignorance in psychic affairs. He won't be able to understand our communicative system."

Perhaps they have raised a valid point. It may be that there is no truly scientific way to test psychic phenomena.

Psychics are fallible, and they recognize this within limits. However, when dealing with their convictions and religious views, they lose all hesitancy — *then* they claim to *know!*

When launching the research for this book, we exposed a group of leading psychics — fifty to be exact — to a basic set of eighty-seven questions. It was our hope that the answers might ultimately reveal the religious convictions of the top psychic teachers and lead us to an understanding of the beliefs of their followers.

We checked their formal church affiliation — Protestant, Catholic, Jewish or other. We marked where their specific activity fit into the psychic world: is he perhaps a clairvoyant? an astrologer? is he a medium or maybe a psychometrist — or both? does he belong also in any of the other categories listed?

Many of these psychics have totally different views as to the origin of the power operating in them. To some it's natural; to others more of a religious force; still others claim to receive the power from spirit entities. Does the psychic believe in spirit communication? Will there be a Second Coming of Christ? Was Christ a man or was He divine? Is the devil an evil being, or is this just a name for a negative force? How about devil worship? Is it really superior to Christianity, as some psychics allege? The validity of the Bible as a guidebook for humanity becomes an issue too.

There are practically no limitations when delving into the operations of the unknown. Because we are concerned with phenomena without definite boundaries, the questions for this kind of research are extremely varied. Examining the psychic mind is not restricted to merely three dimensions, as claimed by the parapsychologists. There is a fourth dimension — religion — for we are dealing with something that manifests much of the same kind of power (though limited) as that expressed by God in the Scriptures. Because of this, we also exposed today's psychics to some of the major tests of true prophets as outlined in the Bible.

Are the biblical prophecies dealing with the end of the world still valid?

In your predictions, do you warn the people of a coming judgment?

Are your predictions in absolute harmony with those written down by the biblical prophets?

Do you point out the sins and transgressions of the people against God?

Do you counsel your church in spiritual matters?

All these questions were among those included in the survey, and they were all answered.

Checking fifty leading psychics in the United States with an impartial, religiously oriented survey — letting *them* do the talking about their beliefs — proved to be one of the most intense and thought-provoking investigations yet.

When this book was still an unharnessed dream, it was decided to categorize the questionnaire into seven specific areas: Personal information, Psychic category, Religious beliefs and convictions, Tests of a true prophet, Reincarnation and flying saucers, Faith healing and astrology, and General information. It resulted in a workable arrangement.

Evaluating the psychics for their religious views produced a different reaction every time. *Only one refused to participate* on the grounds that her knowledge was too sacred to be shared for a mere survey; she strongly voiced her unwillingness to have us compare her God-given ability to that of "those charlatans." Most others were very cooperative.

There was the question of anonymity. One had a contract with a writer that would not allow him to speak openly to another author: "I'll speak, but don't mention my name." Others felt that if the survey did not prove favorable to them, their reputations would suffer irreparable damage . . . hence, no name. Still others objected for more private reasons.

The Soul Hustlers

Inasmuch as the majority of the interviews were done by phone and recorded for future evaluation (with the permission of the psychics), they all remained faceless. Going one step further — eliminating all their names from the survey — also aided in the total evaluation, as it erased the possible appeal of a noted personality. In some cases it was impossible to conduct the interview; therefore the facts had to be gleaned from previously collected information and taped reports already on file. For example, as regards Jeane Dixon, old files were extracted to obtain the hard-core information, and recent tape-recorded interviews were borrowed from a fellow journalist to enable us to analyze the vocal statements on the PSE.

To make this project more than just a survey, we requested vocal answers on a yes or no basis; to be recorded for transfer to computer sheets and for use with the Psychological Stress Evaluator. Have you ever tried to answer a questionnaire with only affirmative or negative reactions? I admit that a strictly positive or negative response does not always result in clear answers to philosophical or religious questions; however, most psychics tend to think carefully before giving such a narrow response, and more often than not, the answer contains the condensed essence of their thinking.

Recorded over a span of several months, the interviews are marked with spiked answers.

"Second coming of Christ? You wonder whether this will ever happen?" one psychic countered. "Horsefeathers!"

Others were more considerate in their replies. Throughout the interviews, I became increasingly aware that even though the various occultists are in the same camp, they react as individuals having their own specific life styles, experiences, and dislikes. When asked whether the devil is an evil being, one psychic responded, *"The devil, sir, is dead! He was indeed an evil being, but is no longer. He was active until a few years ago when he was transmuted into another body!"*

Further into the interview, the same person was asked whether Satan can heal also, and the reply was instantaneous: "Yes, I believe that he can heal indeed!"

A contradiction, you say? Yes, it most certainly was, but that is what this book is all about.

Judging from the cooperation I received, I conclude that the psychics feel they have nothing to hide. Perhaps a clue to this confidence lies in one prediction made to me by a clairvoyant during our interview.

"Around the end of this century," he said solemnly, *"there will be a great war destroying about 90 percent of all the people on earth. The remaining 10 percent will witness the end of the world!"*

His answers, too, are now stored in the computer.

Notes

[1]*National Tattler*, 28 July 1974.

[2]*National Enquirer*, 4 February 1975.

[3]*Beware Familiar Spirits*, 1938, p. 83.

[4]*The Teachings and Phenomena of Spiritualism*, p. 72.

[5]Hans Holzer, *The Directory of the Occult* (Chicago: Henry Regnery Co., 1974), p. 5.

[6]Daniel Logan, *The Reluctant Prophet* (New York: Avon Books, 1971), p. 227.

The Electronic Probe

3

3   The Electronic Probe

3 "AND HE SAID UNTO ME, IT IS DONE. I am Alpha and Omega, the beginning and the end. I will give unto him that is athirst of the fountain of the water of life freely.

"He that overcometh shall inherit all things; and I will be his God, and he shall be my son.

"But the fearful, and unbelieving, and the abominable, and murderers, and whoremongers, and sorcerers, and idolaters, and all liars, shall have their part in the lake which burneth with fire and brimstone: which is the second death" (Rev. 21:6-8).

What do the psychic practitioners profess to believe?

Thus far it has been nearly impossible to ascertain with any reliability the degree to which supernormal manifestations have penetrated nominal Christianity; but now, thanks to the magic power of the computer, we are able to ascertain to some degree the extent of occultic infiltration of the institutional church.

The computer can tabulate the results of an investigation, but it cannot set the standards. They must be programmed into its electronic circuitry. We have to supply the guidelines against which the various phenomena of the twentieth century can be measured. Because a manifestation seems strange and illusory, we cannot always assume that it is ungodly and should be relegated to the sphere of devilish influence.

The controversy between Christ and Satan is older than the dawn of history, but is not necessarily without definite demarcation lines.

As the ultimate guidebook for evaluating supernormal events, the Bible contains a wealth of counsel. From Genesis to Revelation, from the first book — where Satan's beguiling entry in the Garden of Eden is described — to the last book of the Bible, a solid line of supernatural guidance runs from chapter to chapter, giving counsel, evaluating, and warning the human race.

But it contains more than just that. It sets off the boundaries between godly direction and satanic interference in human affairs. It charts the supreme standards of godly inspiration against which all ungodly manifestations can be measured. The computer may be our measuring tool; the Bible is the absolute norm of perfection.

All practitioners of the supernatural operating today employ techniques that are reminiscent of biblical manifestations — that is, the psychics prophesy; the faith healers claim to work with godly power; astrologers proudly point to the celestial bodies as God-ordained tools for foretelling future events; clairvoyants are reputed to have "spiritual" insight; mediums boast of having contact with supernatural beings. Even psychometrists, palmists, witches, and devil worshipers are now saying that their power comes from a pure and holy source and is totally beyond critique.

In varying degrees, they all allege to have a certain amount of godly power driving them. Because of this, the Bible can become the standard for judging their activities. It is God's "code of ethics," and whatever does not conform to its strict and absolute requirements must be condemned.

The Electronic Probe

What is more logical than to pitch their claims against this Absolute Norm and see whether the 53 percent of Americans who are psychically oriented are indeed influenced by a godly force?

Psychics have a unique way of evaluating their gift which is largely governed by their insecurity and chronic unhappiness. Some of them would give anything to be "normal" — at least so they say — because they exist in an enclosure of uncertainty resulting from an ability they neither understand nor control.

Others have standing appointments with their psychiatrists, hoping that costly counseling sessions will erase their dissatisfaction. "Many of them suffer from psychosomatic illnesses," one psychiatrist told me in confidence without divulging the names of his clients. "They feel haunted by both gift and followers, and when the financial rewards are not what they expect them to be — brother, watch out!"

It is no wonder that a great number of them were irritated or confused, although cooperative, when they were confronted with the psychic survey. Not only did it probe deeper, beyond the threshold of contentment, but it required them to evaluate the basis of their own thinking, their beliefs, and to translate the essence of their philosophy or conviction into either a "yes" or a "no" reaction.

While the entire Soul Hustlers Survey contained eighty-seven questions, many of them dealt with nonreligious issues, such as personal background, marital status, age, and so on. Detailed questions pertaining to reincarnation and flying saucers also diverged from some of the hard-core questions. Thirty-one, however, are basic to a Christian's faith, and their response to these were indicative of the contradictions that exist between psychic faith and biblical teaching.

The statistical table recounting survey results (pages 67-71) provides data in eight categories of psychics. Some of the fifty psychics interviewed placed themselves in more than one category, and this is reflected in the statistics. The eight categories are defined thus:

The Soul Hustlers

Psychic prophet — Someone able to forecast events based on supernatural information received from an ungodly source.

Faith healer — A healer who bases the healing of the sick on a strengthening of a supposedly inherent psychic ability of man, not necessarily through the power of Christ. These psychic healers are to be distinguished from evangelical Christian faith healers, who have not been polled in this survey.

Astrologer — Someone who claims to find supernatural guidance through study of the heavenly bodies and who believes our future is predetermined by the planets.

Clairvoyant — A medium who has the ability to "see" into a person's life, giving us details usually known only to the subject.

Medium — Usually identified as a person who professes to be the go-between for man and entities residing in the spirit world. They claim the ability to contact the spirits of the dead.

Psychometrists — A person who receives supernatural information about a person by holding or fingering an object belonging to the subject, with or without the person present.

Witch — Someone who believes in the power of witchcraft and claims agency for that power.

Devil worshiper — A person who regards the power of Satan as supreme and who consciously worships him as god.

The following is a commentary on the most significant questions in the survey. The statistical table does not include the questions relating to personal information such as age, name, and locality.

TABLE 2

PSYCHIC CATEGORY (% affirmative)

QUESTION	Psychics	Faith H.	Astrol.	Clairv.	Medium	Psychom.	Witch	Devil Worsh.
Are psychic phenomena religious phenomena?	52.4	58.8	64.3	54.2	50.0	56.5	25.0	40.0
Are psychic phenomena natural phenomena?	71.4	70.6	50.0	66.7	75.0	69.6	100.0	80.0
Do you believe in life during death?	100.0	100.0	100.0	95.8	100.0	100.0	100.0	100.0
Do you believe in the actual second coming of Christ?	33.3	23.5	28.6	25.0	18.7	30.4	25.0	20.0
Do you believe the devil is an evil being/power?	23.8	23.5	35.7	25.0	12.5	21.7	25.0	40.0
Do you believe God is a holy being?	66.7	64.7	57.1	66.7	56.2	65.2	25.0	40.0
Do you believe in God as the Creator?	66.7	58.8	50.0	58.3	43.7	56.5	25.0	40.0
Was Christ a superpsychic human being?	76.2	82.4	64.3	66.7	68.7	69.6	75.0	80.0
Do you believe psychics and mediums have a legitimate place in religious life?	90.5	100.0	92.9	87.5	87.5	95.7	75.0	80.0
Do you believe in astrology?	85.7	94.1	100.0	83.3	93.7	91.3	100.0	100.0
Is there a cosmic battle between Christ and Satan?	33.3	23.5	35.7	29.2	18.7	30.4	25.0	20.0
Are you a spiritualist?	23.8	35.3	35.7	29.2	43.7	34.8	25.0	20.0
Can a true psychic duplicate the wonders wrought by Christ?	81.0	94.1	92.9	79.2	87.5	87.0	100.0	100.0
Is the phenomenon of spiritualism (spiritism) godly?	76.2	94.1	78.6	75.0	81.2	82.6	50.0	60.0
Will psychic phenomena become a guiding factor in national affairs?	95.2	100.0	100.0	91.7	93.7	100.0	100.0	100.0

	Psychics	Faith H.	Astrol.	Clairv.	Medium	Psychom.	Witch	Devil Worsh.
Do you favor complete religious freedom for everyone?	90.5	100.0	92.9	87.5	93.7	95.6	75.0	80.0
Are you inspired by God in your psychic work?	66.7	70.6	57.1	66.7	62.5	73.9	50.0	40.0
Is Satan worship superior to Christianity?	14.3	11.8	21.4	12.5	12.5	17.4	75.0	60.0
Is it possible for a psychic to be led by God and by the devil?	38.1	29.4	35.7	37.5	37.5	43.5	50.0	40.0
Tests of a True Prophet								
Is the Bible a valid guidebook for humanity?	57.1	52.9	42.9	54.2	37.5	47.8	25.0	40.0
Are the biblical prophecies dealing with the end of the world still valid?	23.8	23.5	28.6	29.2	31.2	30.4	25.0	20.0
In your predictions do you warn the people of God's coming judgment?	19.0	23.5	21.4	20.8	31.2	21.7	25.0	20.0
Do you point out the sins and transgressions of the people against God?	28.6	17.6	35.7	29.2	25.0	30.4	25.0	20.0
Do you counsel and advise your church in spiritual matters?	33.3	35.3	42.9	37.5	43.7	39.1	75.0	80.0
Are the psychics with a high rate of accuracy to be regarded as prophets of God?	66.7	82.4	71.4	62.5	68.7	69.6	50.0	60.0
Reincarnation and Flying Saucers (UFOs)								
Do you believe in reincarnation?	81.0	82.4	85.7	70.8	81.2	82.6	100.0	80.0
Do you believe that you have been reincarnated?	81.0	82.4	85.7	70.8	81.2	82.6	100.0	80.0

	Psychics	Faith H.	Astrol.	Clairv.	Medium	Psychom.	Witch	Devil Worsh.
Were all your reincarnations here on earth?	52.4	47.1	57.1	41.7	37.5	52.2	75.0	60.0
Do you believe that there are other inhabited planets?	95.2	94.1	92.9	91.7	93.7	95.7	100.0	100.0
Do you believe that they are inhabited by holy, sinless beings?	61.9	70.6	64.3	62.5	62.5	69.6	50.0	60.0
Do you believe in the existence of flying saucers (UFOs)?	90.5	94.1	100.0	91.7	93.7	95.7	100.0	100.0
Have we been visited by beings from other planets?	85.7	94.1	100.0	87.5	93.7	91.3	100.0	100.0
Are the unidentified flying objects piloted by these beings from other planets?	90.5	94.1	100.0	91.7	93.7	95.7	100.0	100.0
Have you ever seen a UFO?	61.9	58.8	78.6	62.5	56.2	60.9	100.0	100.0
Have you ever been inside a UFO?	28.6	11.8	42.9	29.2	25.0	30.4	100.0	80.0
Did you receive psychic forecasts of the appearances of UFOs?	52.4	47.1	64.3	54.2	62.5	56.5	100.0	80.0
Have you ever been in personal contact with the crew of a UFO?	47.6	52.9	64.3	54.2	62.5	52.2	100.0	100.0
Do you believe that Christ came to us in a UFO?	38.1	58.8	35.7	41.7	56.2	43.5	50.0	60.0
Are these UFO beings more advanced than we are?	85.7	88.2	92.9	87.5	87.5	91.3	100.0	100.0
Faithhealing and Astrology								
Do you believe that psychic healings will become an accepted part of the medical profession?	90.5	94.1	100.0	87.5	93.7	95.7	100.0	100.0
Do you believe that all faithhealing originates with God?	61.9	52.9	64.3	58.3	50.0	65.2	50.0	40.0

	Psychics	Faith H.	Astrol.	Clairv.	Medium	Psychom.	Witch	Devil Worsh.
Do you believe that the devil can heal also?	28.6	29.4	35.7	29.2	31.2	26.1	75.0	80.0
Is astrology as important as biblical prophecy in foretelling the future?	61.9	64.7	78.6	66.7	75.0	69.6	100.0	100.0
Is the biblical condemnation of psychics and astrologers still valid today?	28.6	35.3	21.4	20.8	25.0	26.1	25.0	40.0
Personal Information								
Have you always been psychic?	81.0	70.6	85.6	75.0	68.7	73.9	75.0	80.0
Was your father psychic?	47.6	35.3	57.1	45.8	31.2	47.8	75.0	80.0
Was your mother psychic?	66.7	47.1	64.3	62.5	62.5	69.6	75.6	60.0
Do you have any other relatives who are psychic?	52.4	41.2	35.7	50.0	62.5	47.8	50.0	40.0
Are you Protestant?	52.4	58.8	50.0	54.2	62.5	56.5	50.0	40.0
Are you Catholic?	33.3	29.4	28.6	29.2	25.0	30.4	50.0	40.0
Are you married?	76.2	76.5	85.7	75.0	68.7	73.9	75.0	80.0
Have you ever been divorced?	28.6	35.3	28.6	29.2	31.2	30.4	25.0	40.0
General Information								
Are you able to predict things for yourself?	85.7	88.2	85.7	79.2	81.2	78.3	75.0	80.0
Do you put any faith in predictions made by other psychics?	100.0	94.1	92.9	91.7	100.0	100.0	100.0	80.0
Do you believe that the same source of inspiration can give different psychics different predictions about the same event?	52.4	58.8	57.1	54.2	68.7	56.4	50.0	40.0
Do you have psychic information leading you to believe that we will experience an invasion from outer space in our lifetime?	61.9	58.8	87.5	66.7	62.5	65.2	75.0	80.0

	Psychics	Faith H.	Astrol.	Clairv.	Medium	Psychom.	Witch	Devil Worsh.
Do you use spirit communication in your psychic work?	76.2	82.4	85.7	75.0	81.2	78.3	75.0	80.0
Do you ever consult the predictions of the French astrologer Nostradamus in your work?	28.6	35.3	35.7	33.3	43.7	34.8	25.0	20.0
Will the second coming of Christ coincide with the end of the world?	19.0	17.6	14.3	25.0	25.0	26.1	25.0	20.0
Have you seen this or a similar event already in a vision?	38.1	35.3	57.1	43.5	43.7	43.5	25.0	20.0
Do you feel we should have national laws governing weekly days of religious observance?	19.0	23.5	42.9	30.4	31.2	26.1	50.0	60.0
Do you favor an alliance of all religions?	52.4	52.9	57.1	56.5	56.2	52.2	25.0	40.0
Many psychics have predicted that the end of the world will come at the end of this century. Do you agree?	52.4	58.8	57.1	56.5	56.2	56.5	75.0	80.0
Are you convinced that women have a greater psychic ability than men?	42.9	58.7	57.1	47.8	62.5	47.8	50.0	60.0
Do you believe that witchcraft should be tolerated?	89.9	100.0	85.7	69.6	87.5	73.9	100.0	80.0
Do you believe that a total acceptance of psychic phenomena will lead to a utopia?	81.0	88.2	85.7	82.6	81.2	87.0	100.0	100.0

Do you believe in life during death?

The reaction of the psychic teachers scores a full 100 percent in favor of this belief. This question was not directed to determine their philosophy to life *after* death — a belief on which there is dissent within various Protestant denominations — but the existence of life *during* death. The Bible is very clear on this issue.

Christ said in John 11:11-14, "These things said he: and after that he saith unto them, Our friend Lazarus sleepeth; but I go, that I may awake him out of sleep.

"Then said his disciples, Lord, if he sleep, he shall do well.

"Howbeit Jesus spake of his death: but they thought that he had spoken of taking of rest in sleep.

"Then said Jesus unto them plainly, Lazarus is dead."

In Acts 2:27-29, Luke comments on the same point: "Because thou wilt not leave my soul in hell, neither wilt thou suffer thine Holy One to see corruption.

"Thou has made known to me the ways of life; thou shalt make me full of joy with thy countenance.

"Men and brethren, let me freely speak unto you of the patriarch David, that he is both dead and buried, and his sepulchre is with us unto this day."

There is life *after death*, but the dead certainly do not return to haunt us with revelations and prophecies.

Do you believe in the actual second coming of Christ?

The concepts of this range widely from a spiritual Second Coming, the philosophy of Secret Rapture, no coming at all, or an actual physical return of Christ. The psychics score extremely low on this. As a unit, only 24 percent in the eight groups listed on the chart believe in Christ's second coming. Mediums rank lowest with only 18.7. Even admitted devil worshipers score higher — perhaps because their master knows the true facts.

What does the Bible say? Christ gives us the answer personally in Matthew 24:30,31: "And then shall appear the sign of the Son of man in heaven: and then shall all the tribes of the earth mourn, and they shall see the Son of man coming in the clouds of heaven with power and great glory."

In addition, the apostle John, writing the Revelation from his prison quarters on the Isle of Patmos, witnessed this coming in vision. "Behold, he cometh with clouds," John wrote, "and every eye shall see him, and they also which pierced him: and all kindreds of the earth shall wail because of him. Even so, Amen" (Rev. 1:7).

Do you believe the devil is an evil being/power?

In checking the computer run of psychic answers on this question, it appears that even though the total percentage of nonbelief is only 24, the mediums again rank the lowest with 12.5 percent. *Only 12.5 out of 100 mediums believe that the devil is an evil being.* His top agents (devil worshipers) know better; they at least admit it at a rate of 40 out of 100. Every psychic category scores low on this question; they all express a definite incredulity that there is an evil being manipulating mankind.

Again, inasmuch as they all tread on biblical grounds, the scriptural answers must be considered. There are numerous Bible texts which give us God's evaluation of the devil.

"And there was war in heaven: Michael and his angels fought against the dragon, and the dragon fought and his angels, And prevaileth not; neither was their place found any more in heaven.

"And the great dragon was cast out, that old serpent, called the Devil, and Satan, which deceiveth the whole world; he was cast out into the earth, and his angels were cast out with him" (Rev. 12:7-9).

"Be sober, be vigilant; because your adversary the devil, as a roaring lion, walketh about, seeking whom he may devour" (1 Peter 5:8).

God's Book calls the devil a *deceiver*, a *murderer*, the *father of lies*, an *adversary*, who goes around "seeking whom he may devour." Surely by not acknowledging either the devil's true nature or his self-proclaimed mission as a destroyer, the psychics have alienated themselves from God's cause.

Do you believe God is a holy being?

Only 64 of every 100 psychics regard the Lord as a holy being. This is certainly a low percentage for people who claim to be filled with the power of God, which again indicates the tremendous difference existing between these professed followers of Christ and what the Bible teaches. I do not count on the psychics being fervid Bible students; however, if they are as close to God as they would have us believe, then we must expect a reasonable understanding of the attributes of God.

Listen to God describe His nature to us.

"For I am the LORD your God: ye shall therefore sanctify yourselves, and ye shall be holy; for I am holy: neither shall you defile yourselves with any manner of creeping thing that creepeth upon the earth.

"For I am the LORD that bringeth you up out of the land of Egypt, to be your God: ye shall therefore be holy, for I am holy" (Lev. 11:44,45).

"And the four beasts had each of them six wings about him: and they were full of eyes within: and they rest not day and night, saying Holy, holy, Lord God Almighty, which was, and is, and is to come" (Rev. 4:8).

God is holy, and just because the psychics do not credit Him with this unique property does not make Him any less holy or distinct.

Do you believe in God as the Creator?

The survey indicates that even fewer believe in this than in the previous question. The evolutionary theory combined with a disbelief in the power of God has undoubtedly penetrated the ranks of the psychics. Fifty-six out of every 100 accept God as the Creator; 44 others deny Him that distinction.

Here too their opinion is in clear contradiction to the Word of God. Moses said in Genesis 1:1, "In the beginning God created the heaven and the earth."

The psalmist echoed the words of Moses: "For all the gods of the nations are idols: but the LORD made the heavens" (Ps. 96:5).

The prophet Jeremiah reemphasized these texts and with pathos and feeling wrote, "He hath made the earth by his power, he hath established the world by his wisdom, and hath stretched out the heavens by his discretion.

"When he uttereth his voice, there is a multitude of waters in the heavens, and he causeth the vapours to ascend from the ends of the earth; he maketh lightnings with rain, and bringeth forth the wind out of his treasures" (Jer. 10:12,13).

God's Book, His prophets, His spokesmen all reassure us that God is master, not only of this creation but of the elements as well. Can we honestly assume that the 56 percent who claim to have faith in God genuinely believe in Him?

Was Christ a superpsychic human being?

Many psychics are convinced of this. When interviewed concerning this question, 72 percent claimed that Christ was a superpsychic.[1] They place His ability to perform the supernatural in the realm of human development, not godly power.

With touching eloquence, the apostle John introduces Him as the Lord of Creation in the first three verses of his Gospel: "In the beginning was the Word, and the Word was with God, and the Word was God. The same was in the beginning with God. All things were made by him; and without him was not any thing made that was made" (1:1-3).

Does this sound like the work of a mere human being?

In Hebrews 1:8, the apostle Paul further defines the role of Christ: "But unto the Son he saith, Thy throne, O God, is for ever and ever: a sceptre of righteousness is the sceptre of thy kingdom." And in verse 10: "And, Thou, Lord, in the beginning hast laid the foundation of the earth; and the heavens are the work of thine hands."

The erroneous assertion that Christ was a human being endowed with extraordinary psychic ability is of spiritualist origin and has no place in Bible-based Christianity. The psychics know this — but have chosen to ignore it. Promulgating the misconception that Christ is *not* the Son of God, but "one of us," is a flagrant violation of Christian doctrine, which God certainly cannot excuse.

Do you believe psychics and mediums have a legitimate place in religious life?

More than 90 percent of all psychic seers and 100 percent of psychic faith healers confidently replied to this question in the affirmative. In fact, the average score of the eight groups together is 92 percent, which indicates that, not only do they claim to be inspired by the Christian God, but they also want us to accept their work as divine, with an established role in the Christian community. A quick look at their performance and their violation of the tests of true prophets testifies to their fallacious thinking.

Why include faith healers in this list? The total tabulation produced by the computer reveals that the average psychic faith healer does *not* believe in the second coming of Christ, doubts God's creative ability, calls Christ a super-psychic human being, and exercises a strong belief in astrology — all factors that place them in direct contradiction to Christian principles. This does not imply that true faith healing cannot occur. God has the undeniable power to heal, *but when a healer does not meet biblical standards,* should we then believe that his ability is nevertheless godly? Can we claim help from One whose power we deny? It is for this reason that psychic faith healers are included here, for the majority of them definitely are disciples of another master.

Earlier in this book we judged their gifts according to God's strict guidelines as laid down in Deuteronomy 18:9-14. It is a damning judgment of God:

"When thou art come into the land which the LORD thy God giveth thee, thou shalt not learn to do after the abominations of those nations.

"There shall not be found among you any one that maketh his son or his daughter to pass through the fire, or that useth divination, or an observer of times, or an enchanter, or a witch, Or a charmer, or a consulter with familiar spirits, or a wizard, or a necromancer.

"For all that do these things are an abomination unto the LORD: and because of these abominations the LORD thy God doth drive them out from before thee.

"Thou shalt be perfect with the LORD thy God. For these nations, which thou shalt possess, hearkened unto observers of times, and unto diviners: but as for thee, the LORD thy God hath not suffered thee so to do."

If God warned His people centuries ago to refrain from associating with those who indulged in these heathen practices, then these same warnings are still valid today. God is unchangeable, . . . "the same yesterday, and to day, and for ever" (Heb. 13:8).

Do you believe in astrology?

With astrologers, devil worshipers, and witches admitting that they support astrology without reservation, we must concede that it has finally bridged the gap of the ages and once again become a modern fad. Millions of Americans now rely on astrological forecasts, the "observing of times" and persist in it regardless of biblical counsel. Of all the occult practitioners polled, 88 percent express faith in this Chaldean institution, which is examined in chapter 7 of this book.

Both Jeremiah and Isaiah provided explicit advice on the subject.

"Hear ye the word which the LORD speaketh unto you, O house of Israel," warned Jeremiah. "Thus saith the LORD, Learn not the way of the heathen, and be not dismayed at the signs of heaven; for the heathen are dismayed at them" (Jer. 10:1,2).

The Soul Hustlers

"Thou art wearied in the multitude of thy counsels," said Isaiah. "Let now the astrologers, the stargazers, the monthly prognosticators, stand up, and save thee from these things that shall come upon thee.

"Behold, they shall be as stubble; the fire shall burn them; they shall not deliver themselves from the power of the flame: there shall not be a coal to warm at, nor fire to sit before it" (Isa. 47:13,14).

Is there a cosmic battle between Christ and Satan?

In all, 24 percent of the psychic practitioners deny this possibility. Scoring the lowest with 20 percent are the mediums, with the devil worshipers a close second. Only 23.5 percent of the faith healers express belief in this biblical doctrine.

Paul, in the Epistle to the Ephesians, wrote about this battle repeatedly: "Wherein in time past ye walked according to the course of this world, according to the prince of the power of the air, the spirit that now worketh in the children of disobedience" (2:2).

"Put on the whole armour of God," Paul continued in 6:11,12, "that ye may be able to stand against the wiles of the devil. For we wrestle not against flesh and blood, but against principalities, against powers, against the rulers of darkness of this world, against spiritual wickedness in high places."

Can a true psychic duplicate the wonders wrought by Christ?

Considering that psychics work with satanic power and that the devil is not God's equal in any way, we have to disclaim this assumption. Yet Satan comes incredibly close to performing wonders and miracles through which many are ensnared.

Listen to Paul in the Second Epistle to the Corinthians: "And no marvel; for Satan himself is transformed into an angel of light. Therefore it is no great thing if his ministers also be transformed as the ministers of righteousness; whose end shall be according to their works" (11:14,15).

Paul raised the likelihood that Satan's ministers will operate while appearing as godly men and will attempt to imitate God's children. In Matthew 24, Christ warned that false prophets would deceive many (v. 11) and that they would perform great signs and wonders . . . great, yes, but not duplicates of those wrought by Christ.

The most sensitive area concerning this is faith healing. We know that God loves His created beings, yet allows suffering to happen. We can assume disease is caused either by Satan or by the weakness of man's fallen nature or by a continuing violation of principles of good health. When someone who claims to possess the godly gift of healing "performs" a miracle, this does not necessarily prove that this healing is a godly act. According to the survey, the majority of today's healers do not adhere to orthodox biblical principles; why then should God use them as His instruments?

Every healing and every miraculous occurrence is not always the result of godly intervention.

Is the phenomenon of spiritualism (spiritism) godly?

In counseling His people during their sojourn in the Sinai Desert, God directed their paths with means of total guidance. This included rules not only for healthful living, but also for the various aspects of their religious life. Because of His desire to safeguard them from indulging in satanic manifestations, He warned them against specific phenomena which had been adopted by the heathen tribes surrounding them, yet were not of godly origin. Some of God's strongest admonitions were aimed at these devilish manifestations:

"Ye shall not eat any thing with the blood; neither shall ye use enchantment, nor observe times. . . . Regard not them that have familiar spirits, neither seek after wizards, to be defiled by them: I am the LORD your God" (Lev. 19: 26,31).

And in Leviticus 20:27, He said, "A man also or woman

that hath a familiar spirit, or that is a wizard, shall surely be put to death: they shall stone them with stones: their blood shall be upon them."

The phenomena mentioned here are those we are encountering today. "Enchantment" is witchcraft; "observing of times" is the ancient designation for astrology. Someone who has a "familiar spirit" is (a medium) one who claims to be guided by a spirit. The "wizard" spoken of in the Bible is the clairvoyant or psychic.

Can these manifestations of power be godly if He Himself condemns to death their practitioners? "To the law and to the testimony" it states in Isaiah 9:20, "if they speak not according to this word, it is because there is no light in them."

Are you inspired by God in your psychic work?

Sixty-one percent of the occult operators believe they are inspired by God — but they are unable to support their conviction with God's Word.

First John 4:1-3 illustrates God's position in regard to their unsubstantiated claims: "Beloved, believe not every spirit, but try the spirits whether they are of God: because many false prophets are gone out into the world.

"Hereby know ye the spirit of God: Every spirit that confesseth that Jesus Christ is come in the flesh is of God: And every spirit that confesseth not that Jesus Christ is come in the flesh is not of God: and this is that spirit of antichrist, whereof ye have heard that it should come; and even now already is it in the world."

With 72 percent of the occultists professing that Christ was not necessarily the Son of God, but a superpsychic human being instead, it is clear that based on the above scriptures, they are not inspired by God in their psychic work. The condemnation of their practices becomes even more evident when their other violations to God's counsel are added to this presumptuous claim.

Is Satan worship superior to Christianity?

The table indicates that the various groups have decidedly different opinions on this question, affirmation coming from 75 percent of the witches and only 11.8 percent of the faith healers. Living in a nominally Christian society, we may find it difficult to imagine that at the present time literally millions of Americans unwittingly worship Satan rather than God.

" . . . I am the way, the truth, and the life: no man cometh unto the Father, but by me," counseled Christ in John 14:6.

To this the apostle Paul added in Galatians 1:7,8, "But there be some that trouble you, and would pervert the gospel of Christ. But though we, or an angel from heaven, preach any other gospel unto you than that which we have preached unto you, *let him be accursed.*"

Worshiping Satan, the adversary of Christ, cannot be superior to Christianity. Inwardly many psychics are cognizant of this, which perhaps accounts for the widespread variation in conviction on this point.

Is it possible for a psychic to be led by God and by the devil?

Sixty-eight out of every 100 teachers of the occult believe this is possible. They try to align themselves with both God and the devil, a contributory factor as to why their religious thinking and their prophetic work is in such disarray.

The clearest refutation to their claim comes from Christ's answer to the Pharisees who confronted Him after a healing miracle.

In Matthew 12, Jesus pointed out the results of a conscious division of allegiance:

"And Jesus knew their thoughts, and said unto them, Every kingdom divided against itself is brought to desolation; and every city or house divided against itself shall not stand. . . .

"He that is not with me is against me; and he that gathereth not with me scattereth abroad. . . .

"Either make the tree good, and his fruit good; or else

make the tree corrupt, and his fruit corrupt: for the tree is known by his fruit. . . .

"A good man out of the good treasure of the heart bringeth forth good things: and an evil man out of the evil treasure bringeth forth evil things" (vv. 25,30,33,35).

Obviously Christ does not allow for the possibility of divided allegiance. Either we are *for* Him or *against* Him. Here too the psychic position is unbiblical.

Is the Bible a valid guidebook for humanity?

There are about twenty tests of a true prophet applicable to today's prognosticators in order to establish their degree of godliness. The five tests included in the survey are among the essential ones, but are nevertheless disregarded by the psychics, revealing once more the magnitude of their offenses against God.

Less than 50 percent (precisely 48 percent) of these polled for the survey no longer believe in the infallibility of the Bible; however, they perpetuate the allegation that they are being led by God.

Two Bible passages especially attest to the inspiration and absoluteness of the Scriptures:

"All scripture is given by inspiration of God, and is profitable for doctrine, for reproof, for correction, for instruction in righteousness" (2 Tim. 3:16).

We have also a more sure word of prophecy; whereunto ye do well that ye take heed, as unto a light that shineth in a dark place, until the day dawn, and the day star arise in your hearts: "Knowing this first, that no prophecy of the scripture is of any private interpretation. For the prophecy came not in old time by the will of man: but holy men of God spake as they were moved by the Holy Ghost" (2 Peter 1: 19-21).

The Bible has not lost any of its validity, for it has been inspired by an unchangeable God. It is still a reliable guidebook for the human race.

The Electronic Probe

Are the biblical prophecies dealing with the end of the world still valid?

In talking to proponents of anti-Christian doctrines, I find that the end-of-the-world concept as taught in the Scriptures is a point of truth that becomes less significant with each passing year. Those psychics, faith healers, mediums, and others who claim to have God's guidance in their lives rank almost as low as the avowed devil worshipers in denying the relevance of the prophecies concerning the end of the world.

If we believe the Word of God, we should have no doubt about the impending reality of the end of the world. Says Christ in Matthew 24:35,36, "Heaven and earth shall pass away, but my words shall not pass away. But of that day and hour knoweth no man, no, not the angels of heaven, but my Father only."

The apostle Peter adds in 2 Peter 3:3,4, and 10, "Knowing this first, that there shall come in the last days scoffers, walking after their own lusts, And saying, Where is the promise of his coming? for since the fathers fell asleep, all things continue as they were from the beginning of the creation. . . .

"But the day of the Lord will come as a thief in the night; in the which the heavens shall pass away with a great noise, and the elements shall melt with fervent heat, the earth also and the works that are therein shall be burned up."

Peter foresaw in the final days of earth's history that serious doubts would arise concerning this climactic event, but he also pointed with definitive clarity toward the fulfillment of the prophecies proclaiming the end of the world.

In your predictions do you warn the people of God's coming judgment?

One of the greatest tests of a true biblical prophet was that he met the requirement of warning the people of the coming judgment of God. Listen to the prophets Isaiah and John speak about the role of prophecy as it relates to the admonitions of God:

"The earth is utterly broken down, the earth is clean dissolved, the earth is moved exceedingly.

"The earth shall reel to and fro like a drunkard, and shall be removed like a cottage; and the transgression thereof shall be heavy upon it; and it shall fall, and not rise again. And it shall come to pass in that day, that the Lord shall punish the host of the high ones that are on high, and the kings of the earth upon the earth" (Isa. 24:19-21).

Even angels join in making known this prophecy, wrote John in Revelation 14:6,7: "And I saw another angel fly in the midst of heaven, having the everlasting gospel to preach unto them that dwell on the earth, and to every nation, and kindred, and tongue, and people,

"Saying with a loud voice, Fear God, and give glory to him; for the hour of his judgment is come: and worship him that made heaven, and earth, and the sea, and the fountains of waters."

Both the angels and His prophets proclaim the hour of His judgment. Would God not demand the same of His prophets today even more urgently as the time of the end draws nearer? Yet only 20 percent of the psychics fulfill this requirement.

Do you point out the sins and transgressions of the people against God?

The percentage of psychics and supernatural manipulators who admit to fulfilling this important requisite is only 24 — almost as low as the figure for the previous test. Somehow the ability to forecast the outcome of a horse race or a presidential election seems more essential to them than pointing out the sins and transgressions of humanity.

God, when speaking to the prophet Ezekiel, instructed him to speak in His name.

"Son of man," He addressed Ezekiel, "I have made thee a watchman unto the house of Israel: therefore hear the word at my mouth, and *give them warning from me*" (Ezek. 3:17). It was the Lord's unchangeable word given to His prophet, informing him of his duties to both God and man. It was precise, but not new, for God had given basically the same instruction to His prophet Isaiah more than one hundred years before, when He said,

"Cry aloud, spare not, lift up thy voice like a trumpet, and *shew my people their transgression,* and the house of Jacob their sins" (Isa. 58:1).

The word *prophet* signifies much more than merely foretelling future events. Biblical prophets were spokesmen for God, and in their role as God's ambassadors they were to relay not only His blessings, but His warnings as well.

Do you counsel and advise your church in spiritual matters?

Amazingly enough, even though most of today's prophets claim to be "spokesmen for God," relatively few boast of their affiliation with a church. One-third of the psychic prophets polled said they advise their church; barely more faith healers also admitted that this was part of their function. The mediums scored 43.7 percent, but the greatest percentage on this issue was reached by the witches and devil worshipers, who undoubtedly wield great influence in the various satanic churches that dot the United States. If it were not for the fact that their doctrines are diametrically opposite to godly principles, one might conclude that they almost fulfill God's requirement! Their work, however, is not of godly origin, nor is their advice intended for a church founded on Christian principles.

Ephesians 4:11-13 shows how deeply the spiritual gifts are to affect God's church. Regarding this, 1 Corinthians 14:3,4 also counsels, "But he that prophesieth speaketh unto men to edification, and exhortation, and comfort. He that speaketh in an unknown tongue edifieth himself, *but he that prophesieth edifieth the church.*"

Are the psychics with a high rate of accuracy to be regarded as prophets of God?

This concerns the question of a prophet's accuracy, a concept which all modern seers greatly treasure. An astounding 68 percent of today's prognosticators feel that a high rate of accuracy is sufficient to be classified as "one of God's very own."

During many hourlong discussions I have had with psychics over the years, they have tried to persuade me to accept this. However, biblical evidence proves otherwise. God does not employ part-time envoys: one is either totally on God's side, guided by true inspiration and speaking with 100 percent accuracy; or one is not, in which case the devil takes the credit.

The Lord again issued His warnings regarding false prophets through Moses the lawgiver in the early history of the Hebrews.

"If there arise among you a prophet, or a dreamer of dreams, and giveth thee a sign or a wonder," wrote Moses in Deuteronomy 13:1-5, "And the sign or the wonder come to pass, whereof he spake unto thee, saying, Let us go after other gods, which thou has not known, and let us serve them;

"Thou shalt not hearken unto the words of that prophet, or that dreamer of dreams: . . . And that prophet, or that dreamer of dreams, shall be put to death; because he hath spoken to turn you away from the LORD your God."

Later, speaking through the prophet Jeremiah, God repeated His previous warnings: "The prophet which prophesieth of peace, *when the word of the prophet shall come to pass, then shall the prophet be known, that the Lord has truly sent him*" (Jer. 28:9).

A PAQ (Prophetic Accuracy Quotient) of 85 or even 90 percent just is not enough to be ranked among the men of God. The Lord does not work in percentages.

Do you believe in reincarnation?

Seventy-six percent of all those interviewed admitted that their beliefs include faith in reincarnation. An equal percentage claimed that they had already passed through the process and would again be reincarnated at a future date. Of this group, only 44 percent were confident that they had lived before on this planet: 33 percent were convinced that in a former life, they had existed on other heavenly bodies.

Is there any credence to this? Does the Bible support the idea that we live countless lives, with each one trying to eradicate the mistakes and blunders credited to us from a previous existence? A conscientious combing of the Bible has not uncovered one verse of Scripture in which God remotely suggests the possibility of recycled existence. Instead we read in Job 14:11-14:

"As the waters fail from the sea, and the flood decayeth and drieth up: So man lieth down, and riseth not: till the heavens be no more, they shall not awake, nor be raised out of their sleep.

"O that thou wouldest hide me in the grave, that thou wouldest keep me secret, until thy wrath be past, that thou wouldest appoint me a set time and remember me!

"If a man die, shall he live again?" Job asked in desperation and then furnished the answer: "All the days of my appointed time will I wait, till my change come."

Surely there is no suggestion of reincarnation in this text. Nor is there in Psalm 146:3,4, in which David wrote,

"Put not your trust in princes, nor in the son of man, in whom there is no help. His breath goeth forth, he returneth to his earth; in that very day his thoughts perish."

The Bible is not speaking of reincarnation, but of *creation*.

"Whereas ye know not what shall be on the morrow," James wrote in his epistle, "For what is your life? It is even a vapour, that appeareth for a little time, and then vanisheth away" (4:14). We are *created*, we *die*, we pass through the *judgment* and receive our *eternal reward* or *punishment*, but nowhere in the Bible do we find reincarnation mentioned in relation to any of these. Reincarnation is not built on a biblical foundation, but rather on Eastern philosophy and mediumistic communication.

Do you believe the other inhabited planets are inhabited by holy, sinless beings?

The UFO craze raging throughout the country has given rise to many theories regarding the origin of these craft — the most prevalent being that they are launched from spaceports on other inhabited planets.

For years prominent mediums have claimed to be in contact with these beings. As a result, more than 96 percent of all those indulging in supernormal phenomena are firmly convinced that UFOs are visiting us from outer space. *Yet only 62.5 percent believe these beings are holy.* The Bible maintains that there *are* other created beings beyond earth and indicates that, not 62.5 percent, but *all* are holy:

"Thou, even thou, art LORD alone; thou hast made heaven, the heaven of heavens, with all their host, the earth, and all things that are therein, the seas, and all that is therein, and thou preservest them all; and the host of heaven worshippeth thee" (Neh. 9:6).

"Bless ye the LORD, all ye his hosts; ye ministers of his, that do his pleasure" (Ps. 103:21).

"Take ye therefore good heed unto yourselves; . . . lest thou lift up thine eyes unto heaven, and when thou seest the sun, and the moon, and the stars, even all the host of heaven, shouldest be driven to worship them, and serve them" (Deut. 4:15,19).

Scientific data support the contention that there is indeed intelligent life in our solar system. Modern science has enabled us to penetrate the black unknown of the universe with radio telescopes, so sensitive and so precise that they can pick up cosmic signals from one hundred light-years in space.

Dr. Harlow Shapley, Harvard professor emeritus of astronomy, has worked out some interesting statistics on the *probability* — not just the possibility — of intelligent life in space.

According to his calculations, the number of stars we can "listen" to with our modern radio telescopes can be estimated at the number *10 followed by nineteen zeroes.* "Of this unthinkable number," he was asked, "how many stars have planets rushing about them?" His answer: "One in a thousand." Of these "one-in-a-thousand" worlds, again one in a thousand will lie just the right distance from its sun so that a moderate temperature can sustain life. Of these planets, Dr. Shapley says, one in a thousand will be large enough to bind and keep the atmosphere. He applies his one-in-a-thousand ratio once more when asked how many of this vast reduced number will have the proper atmosphere with the right amounts of hydrogen, nitrogen, carbon, and oxygen to support cellular life such as exists on earth. Subtracting the total number of stars that can be "seen" with the radio telescope this way still leaves us with *one hundred million planets in the universe on which some kind of life is not only possible but probable,* Dr. Shapley concludes.

In 1959, a determined effort was made to try to establish contact with some of these "possible" planets through a new radio telescope constructed at Green Bank, West Virginia. The communications attempt, known as Project Ozma, was aimed at contacting the star Tau Ceti. The distances involved, however, are so enormous that the signal beamed at Tau Ceti in 1959 did not arrive there until 1970, traveling at the speed of light — more than 186,000 miles per second. This means that roughly six years ago, Tau Ceti may have been able to listen in on the first intelligent communication beamed at it from Earth. If there are inhabitants there, and if they took the decision at that time to *answer* us, then we cannot expect their reply until 1981 — again coming at us with a speed of 186,000 miles per second. And this is only one of the 100,000,000 stars in our galaxy believed capable of supporting life as we know it.

I do not at all doubt that we are only a minor, insignificant blot of life in the vast universe. Is it conceivable that God would allow the beings residing on those stars to risk contamination by sin through visiting our planet?

Do you believe that Christ came to us in a UFO?

Among UFO enthusiasts, the story in Ezekiel 1:15-28 of the prophet's vision about the wheel is the first psychic impression of a flying saucer. There have been numerous misinterpretations of this incident, but theologians do not agree on its significance. The Ufologists have gone one step further and now imply that this was the same "vehicle" in which Christ came to earth the first time. Matthew 1:21-25 does not suggest that this was the case, as the Bible clearly teaches that Christ was born of a virgin and was conceived supernaturally. Luke's account states,

"And the angels answered and said unto her, The Holy Ghost shall come upon thee, and the power of the Highest shall overshadow thee: therefore also that holy thing which shall be born of thee shall be called the Son of God" (Luke 1:35).

The Bible refers only to a physical birth, the result of a supernatural conception.

Do you believe that psychic healings will become an accepted part of the medical profession?

For many faith healers and for those who are healed, the idea that not all healings are God-inspired or God-originated is simply preposterous.

"I know what happened to me," they answer, often vehemently. "I know it was the hand of God that healed me."

Feeling is never proof. God requires us to base our belief on facts — on Scriptures — and they indeed support the idea that healings are not always the work of God.

In speaking about endtime events, Christ commented in Matthew 7:22,23, "Many will say to me in that day, Lord, Lord, *have we not prophesied in thy name? and in thy name have cast out devils? and in thy name done many wonderful works?* And then will I profess unto them, I never knew you: depart from me, ye that work iniquity."

Significant is the fact that 92 percent of all psychic practitioners are convinced that their psychic healings will become part of the medical profession and that new healing methods will be introduced in the medical world. However, only 52.9 percent of the psychic faith healers are reasonably certain that God does the healing. Inasmuch as they could choose only between a strict positive or negative response, with the instruction to allow their stronger conviction to rule their choice, this means that nearly half of the faith healers at least *wonder* whether their power may originate from the wrong source!

Revelation 16:13,14 adds to this, "And I saw three unclean spirits like frogs come out of the mouth of the dragon, and out of the mouth of the beast, and out of the mouth of the false prophet.

"For they are the spirits of devils, working miracles, which go forth unto the kings of the earth and of the whole world, to gather them to the battle of that great day of God Almighty."

All faith healing does not originate with God! Certainly a sobering thought.

Is astrology as important as biblical prophecy in foretelling the future?

Sixty-eight percent of psychic practitioners endorse this view, but in many ways the nation's astrologers are not willing to place their heads on the block for this question. Only 78.6 percent of them believe it is as important as the Bible; the others are not that certain. Only the witches and devil worshipers are completely on the side of astrology; all the other "professions" lean toward it, but are not totally persuaded.

Neither is God.

In the Book of Daniel, we read the story of King Nebuchadnezzar's dream and his demand for not only a recall of the dream, but of the interpretation as well. Daniel 2:27,28 gives us God's response to the claims of the astrologers and magicians of ancient Babylon:

"Daniel answered in the presence of the king, and said, The secret which the king hath demanded *cannot the wise men, the astrologers, the magicians, the soothsayers, shew unto the king.*

"But there is a God in heaven that revealeth secrets, and *maketh known to the king Nebuchadnezzar what shall be in the latter days.* Thy dream, and the visions of thy head upon thy bed, are these."

Prophecy in the sense of foretelling the future comes only from the "God in heaven," not from the astrologers who are the biblical "observers of times" condemned by God throughout the Old Testament.

Is the biblical condemnation of psychics and astrologers still valid today?

This question is referring to the verses in Deuteronomy 18:10-12, where God denounces all those who practice the magic arts — including the "observer of times."

"That's the Old Testament," I have overheard astrologers remark. "That was only for a limited period in history. Things are different now."

But are they really?

In Acts 19:18,19, we read the story of the destruction of books on "curious arts," an ancient designation for what is currently known as "psychic practices":

"And many that believed came, and confessed, and shewed their deeds. *Many of them also which used curious arts* brought their books together, and burned them before all men: and they counted the price of them, and found it fifty thousand pieces of silver."

This clause reads literally, "Many of those who were practicing superfluous things," meaning the superstitious magical arts, which were a specialty in Ephesus. There were innumerable magicians and astrologers in that city who carried on a brisk trade in books of divination and stargazing, as well as guides for interpreting dreams and visions. The fifty thousand pieces of silver mentioned in the text denote a substantial fortune. If this, as it has been thought, meant the Greek drachma, it would be worth the equivalent of $5,000 today. In ancient times, a drachma was equal to a day's earnings; therefore, computed on the basis of a current daily wage of $30, it would represent at least $1,500,000. Quite a sum indeed!

To this New Testament condemnation of these arts can be added another passage, extending God's judgment of these practitioners to the end of time: "But the fearful, and unbelieving, and the abominable and murderers, and whoremongers, and *sorcerers*, and idolaters, and all liars, shall have their part in the lake which burneth with fire and brimstone: which is the second death" (Rev. 21:8).

Astrology is fundamental to the art of the sorcerers and as such is totally "off-limits" to a Christian.

Will the second coming of Christ coincide with the end of the world?

Only 20 percent of those interviewed believe this to be the case, with astrologers and faith healers showing the lowest degree of faith in this doctrine.

Christ's answer to this question is as valid today as it was centuries ago when He spoke to His disciples about the signs of the end of the present world order.

"Immediately after the tribulation of those days shall the sun be darkened, and the moon shall not give her light, and the stars shall fall from heaven, and the powers of the heavens shall be shaken," He told them as a preamble to His second coming.

"And then shall appear the sign of the Son of man in heaven: and then shall all the tribes of the earth mourn, and they shall see the Son of man coming in the clouds of heaven with power and great glory.

"And he shall send his angels with a great sound of a trumpet, and they shall gather together his elect from the four winds, from one end of heaven to the other" (Matt. 24:29-31).

The apostle Paul often referred to the second coming of Christ. In 1 Corinthians 15:22-25, he associated the Second

Coming with the resurrection of the dead and the end of the world as we know it:

"For as in Adam all die, even so in Christ shall all be made alive. But every man in his own order: Christ the firstfruits; afterward they that are Christ's at his coming.

"Then cometh the end, when he shall have delivered up the kingdom to God, even the Father; when he shall have put down all rule and all authority and power. For he must reign, till he hath put all enemies under his feet."

Do you favor an alliance of all religions?

Fifty-two percent of the persons interviewed are in favor of this. No one likes to be wrong, especially those who feel their specific interpretation of Bible doctrine is unique and the *only* way to salvation. However, not everyone's vision of Christ is correct. It may appear that way, but a "one world religion" cannot be what Christ had in mind, for this would mean incorporating both good and bad concepts into one all-embracing faith.

In 2 Corinthians 6:14-17, we find the biblical answer to the desire of the masses:

"Be ye not unequally yoked together with unbelievers: for what fellowship has righteousness with unrighteousness? and what communion hath light with darkness? And what concord hath Christ with Belial? or what part hath he that believeth with an infidel?

"And what agreement hath the temple of God with idols? for ye are the temple of the living God; as God hath said, I will dwell in them, and walk in them; and I will be their God, and they shall be my people.

"*Wherefore come out from among them, and be ye separate, saith the Lord,* and touch not the unclean thing; and I will receive you."

Many psychics have predicted that the end of the world will come at the end of this century. Do you agree?

An impressive number of psychic prophets (see chart) have issued dire warnings, all dealing with catastrophic events to take place at the end of this century. Some label it "the end of the world," others refer to it as a time when "the great change" will occur, still more claim that in approximately twenty-five years a cross will appear in the Eastern skies as a prelude to the second coming of Christ. They try to *pinpoint* the moment of Christ's return to earth and position it in a time slot when many of them will no longer be alive and answerable to the failure of this greatest of all predictions.

Only the Bible can supply the truth to this endtime prediction, and in Mark 13:31-33, we read, "Heaven and earth shall pass away: but my words shall not pass away. But of that day and hour knoweth no man, no, not the angels which are in heaven, neither the Son, but the Father.

"Take ye heed, watch and pray: for ye know not when the time is."

This text tells us that even Christ, the Son of God, while on earth did not know the time, nor the hour of His second coming. If God the Father had not yet included His Son in the planning of this final stage in the plan of salvation, can we then expect He would reveal it to an earthly psychic?

Do you believe that a total acceptance of psychic phenomena will lead to a utopia?

A total acceptance of psychic phenomena would mean a total acceptance of satanic principles expressed in manifestations of an ungodly nature. Will this result in a world without strife?

The apostle Peter clearly answered this question in 2 Peter 3:10-13:

"But the day of the Lord will come as a thief in the night; in the which the heavens shall pass away with a great noise, and the elements shall melt with fervent heat, the earth also and the works that are therein shall be burned up.

"Seeing then that all these things shall be dissolved, what manner of persons ought ye to be in all holy conversation and godliness, Looking for and hasting unto the coming of the day of God, wherein the heavens being on fire shall be dissolved, and the elements shall melt with fervent heat?

"Nevertheless we, according to his promise, look for new heavens and a new earth, wherein dwelleth righteousness."

There will be no utopia based on satanic doctrines, but only one built on the righteousness of Christ.

The psychic world does *not* have the answers for the future.

Notes

[1]The question might well have been phrased, "Was Christ *merely* a superpsychic human being?" This would have indicated clearly the psychics' attitudes toward the biblical teaching that Jesus was both human and divine, incarnate by the Holy Spirit. Nevertheless, we might assume that those psychics who regard Jesus as a superpsychic would be disinclined to attribute true godliness to Him.

The Devil's Naked Truth

4

4   The Devil's Naked Truth

4 AS CORROBORATED BY THE SURVEY RE-
sults, the feeling that the majority of psychics speak as if they have been programmed by a higher being grows stronger with
each passing day.

The longer one examines their responses, the more con-
tradictory the comparison of their answers to biblical doctrine appears and the more ludicrous their claims of godly
inspiration become.

The reactions of those participating in the survey were
indeed startling. Are the psychics perhaps programmed in
such a manner that they are able to answer only what they are
"told" to believe? Their responses may seem spontaneous
and unrehearsed, but nevertheless betray a supernatural
influence. Remember, Satan can sway the mind, but
nevertheless cannot manipulate the human system into total
subservience, utterly erasing impressions left there by child-
hood experiences, education, and the continuous working of
the Holy Spirit.

Satan cannot totally override the God-installed controls of the human reasoning mechanism when superimposing his vibrations on the psychic mind. He must rely on the subject's conscious and willful cooperation. We are God's creation; not Satan's. We are made in His image and in His likeness. Satan's aim is to re-create us in his own perverted image; but to accomplish this, he must obliterate all vestiges of this godly resemblance that still abide in fallen man. Only then can he exercise total control.

But this he cannot do! What he *has* been able to achieve, however, is almost as frightening. Yet there are absolute limitations to his ability. It is this failure to remake man in his image that now betrays him.

From watching him manage his agents — the psychic operators that are now ubiquitous and surround us — we have become aware of his power to "blank out" the discriminating properties of the human mind and generate through the larynx sounds that have no resemblance to the medium's natural voice. In many cases, this influence is manifested *through mind control, not voice control,* allowing the medium to use his own natural voice and vocabulary in expressing what he thinks is his own opinion.

If the answers given by an individual in response to questions are in harmony with knowledge stored in the retrieval system of the brain, then the sound emanating from his larynx is free of stress. If, however, the vocalized opinion violates basic knowledge or is based on an unsupported claim, the subconscious reacts by setting up a chain reaction of tension in the human system. When that happens, the voicebox is in trouble!

A number of years ago, I was busily engaged in researching the whereabouts of Noah's ark, a project with which I had been involved since 1946. While engrossed in activities dealing with the 1970 expedition, word reached us in Washington that a young man in New Mexico, while employed as a summer volunteer at the Smithsonian Institution in 1968, claimed he had seen an expedition comprising members of both the National Geographic Society and the Institution return with the body of Noah and secretly lock it in a vault under strict security.

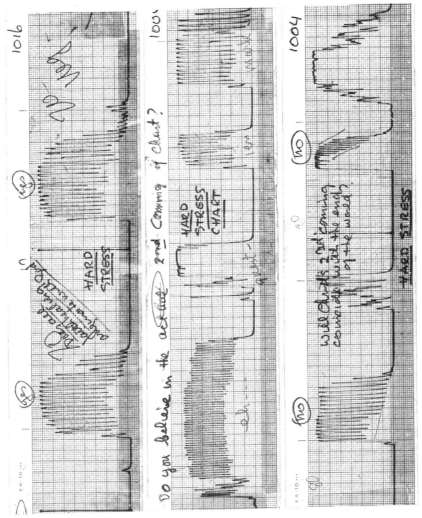

Figure 2. The principle of the PSE is based on the fact that deceitful answers produce areas of *hard stress* on the electrocardiograph tape of the PSE. All the tapes displayed on this and the following pages display the telltale *hard stress* graphs in various degrees, signifying that the subject was under tremendous emotional stress while answering.

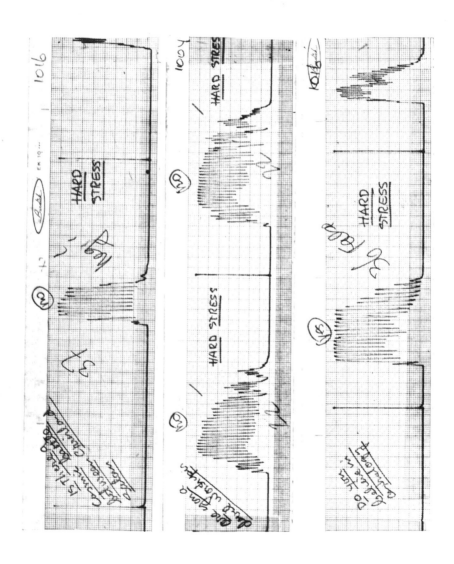

Figure 2a.

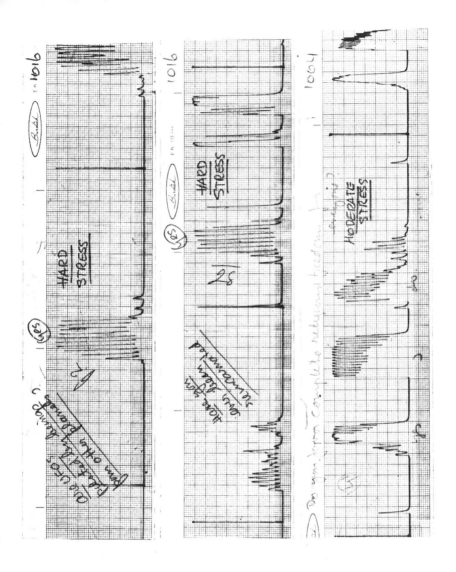

Figure 2b.

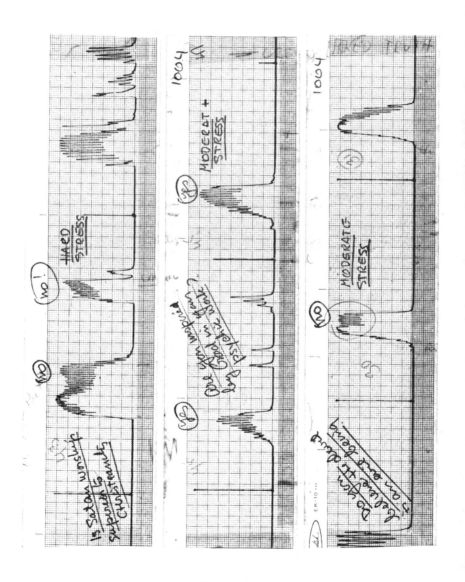

Figure 2c.

The Devil's Naked Truth

The news was intriguing, but also devastating to all those who had sunk thousands of dollars in trying to find the elusive ark and possibly the body of Noah on Mount Ararat in Turkey. The subsequent investigation seemed to confirm an actual discovery until the young man's interviews were subjected to the PSE. The test results showed he had never seen the body of Noah, nor had it been brought to the Smithsonian; yet his story was so convincing that countless ark-researchers were willing to believe him. After all, he had related that same story to many people for several years.

I was reminded of this PSE test when I first began to process the psychic interviews through its circuitry, searching for possible discrepancies between conscious answers and subconscious reactions. The participants were very cooperative, and their replies were usually spontaneous. I had no reason to believe that their answers were not in line with their convictions — but were they perhaps thrust upon their minds by a higher power?

This same question has been raised many times.

Scientific indicators of the actual existence of cosmic intelligences controlling mediums and prophets were supplied by extensive research conducted on Eileen Garrett, one of the world's greatest trance mediums and founder of the Parapsychology Foundation. In her mediumistic work, the now-deceased medium acted under the strict control of an entity calling itself "Uvani."

In spiritualist circles, a trance medium is generally considered to be one of the more advanced practitioners of mediumship. In this situation, it is assumed that a spirit or a ghost has invaded and captured the mind of the unconscious individual and works and speaks through the medium, using his or her voice and body as if it were its own.

While possessed by Uvani, many secrets of people unknown to her during her waking state were brought to the surface; but even though she was informed that these messages came to her from the so-called spirits of the dead, she never felt comfortable with this explanation. Despite her being a primary agent for communications between the unseen entities and this world, Eileen Garrett admitted in her book, *Many Voices: The Autobiography of a Medium*, that she "had never been certain of their reality or that the messages they conveyed from their 'universe' about those who had departed from this life were truly evidence of life after death."[1] She attempted to discover more rational explanations for the phenomenon and concluded that her control personalities were possibly part of her own subconscious.

Hereward Carrington, the late director of the American Psychical Institute, applied a number of specific scientific tests to Mrs. Garrett in order to ascertain whether her subconscious or a definite spirit entity had taken control of her body and voice during her trance state. He utilized the Bernreuter Personality Inventory, the Pages Behaviour Analysis, and other measuring tests which were administered to Mrs. Garrett while in both waking *and* trance states.

The results were startling. The scores of the medium when tested in a normal state, and of Uvani, her control — who was tested while the medium was in a trance state — revealed significant divergence in emotional stability and other factors and indicated *that Carrington was indeed dealing with two different personalities.*

But his research went a step further.

The discovery that Mrs. Garrett's attitude toward church-related questions showed "favorable with reservations" and that Uvani's score showed a "wavering attitude" toward religion motivated Carrington to test both her and Uvani with the conventional lie detector.

In an earlier chapter I explained the operational basis for the PSE, the electronic machine used extensively in the research for this book. The more commonly used lie detector, officially known as the polygraph, which Carrington employed for his investigation, is a device that simultaneously measures and records the various body functions such as heartbeat, blood pressure, respiration rate, and electrical conductivity of the skin. It has received the endorsement of

The Devil's Naked Truth

many researchers and is highly reliable if used by an experienced examiner.

Uvani, Mrs. Garrett's spirit control, willingly allowed himself to be tested with the polygraph. With Mrs. Garrett hooked up to the instrument while in a state of total trance, his responses to questions were recorded on the instrument. Under normal waking conditions, the medium would speak for herself; in trance, the responses were supplied by Uvani.

When Mrs. Garrett's reactions were compared to those of Uvani, they disclosed undeniable differences. Consecutive tests conducted on Mrs. Garrett, Uvani, and other "third" entities resulted in a number of deflections, signifying that they could not have issued from her alone. Carrington's tests revealed that they all differed from each other *fundamentally*.

These reactions then led to other methods of measuring the responses. In a revolutionary experiment, unheard of at that time in psychic research, Dr. Cornelius Traeger, a New York specialist in arthritis and heart disease, administered a series of medical tests to the medium and her "guides," measuring blood count, heart activity, and psychological reactions to various drugs. Commenting on the electrocardiogram and other test results, Dr. Elmer Lindsay, one of Dr. Traeger's colleagues, volunteered, "They were really startling" and "surprising." He further stated that no human heart "could show records so diametrically opposed and divergent."[2]

There is no doubt that supernatural entities do invade human bodies and control them to the extent that they manage to change all their measurable body functions, with different entities creating totally different responses.

For the sake of exposing Satan's true knowledge, we have recorded in table 3 on page 108 the reaction to twelve questions previously tabulated.

It may be difficult to imagine that Satan can control a willing subject so completely, yet he succeeds!

Knowing from previous research that these foreign entities can be detected by electronic means, I began to feed

TABLE 3

Question	A Conscious answers for computer tabulation	B PSE answers showing true reaction of power operating psychics
1. Does all faith healing originate with God?	yes	no
2. Do you believe in the actual second coming of Christ?	no	yes
3. Will Christ's second coming coincide with the end of the World?	no	yes
4. Is there a cosmic battle between Christ and Satan?	no	yes
5. Are you a devil worshiper?	no	yes
6. Do you believe in astrology?	yes	no
7. Are UFOs piloted by beings from other planets?	yes	no
8. Have you ever been reincarnated?	yes	no
9. Do you favor complete religious freedom for everyone?	yes	no
10. Is Satan worship superior to Christianity?	no	yes
11. Are you inspired by God in your psychic work?	yes	no
12. Do you believe the devil is an evil being?	no	yes

the conscious vocal responses I had received from the supernaturalists into the PSE circuitry, searching for answers that might reveal their presence, and in addition, uncover the doctrines they *really* believe in.

Moments after inserting the first response into the instrument, I became aware of substantial stress areas on the chart, created by vocal chords tightened by a subconscious attempt to deceive. The psychic practitioners may have been sincere in their answers to my questions, but what they voiced often violated knowledge stored in their memory cells. When a cross section of the eight groups interviewed was taken, it was evident that although their professed doctrines conflict with known biblical principles, their psychic master knows the difference! The discrepancies are so obvious and so repetitious that it would be an overkill to reproduce all the charted violations.

Those answers listed under **A** on table 3 were voluntarily supplied by the psychics during the tape-recorded interviews for the survey and were included in their *admitted* doctrines and principles of operation. Those ranked under **B** are the PSE revelations given by their voice analysis based on the absence of the telltale microtremors. In this research, the absence or near-absence of these vibrations was so pronounced that we are more than justified in calling the selected answers grossly deceitful. In such instances, we can safely reverse the answers a full 180 degrees. The "yes" becomes a "no" and vice versa.

In the PSE analysis, we find the key to the devil's true feelings. Unable to control completely the medium's subconscious and lock the gate to the microtremors, he unintentionally divulges his real beliefs to us. On every major religion-oriented question, the PSE reaction was extreme, and the charts supply us with a detailed insight into the knowledge Satan attempts to hide.

I have often maintained that in their predictions, psychic prophets are merely mouthpieces for a satanic power and do not act of their own accord. The PSE has now strengthened this viewpoint.

A quick look at the sample list of violations and unintentional admissions show the tremendous contrast that exists between Satan's public claims and his true feelings. He still believes in God — of that there is no doubt. Even the Bible confirms this: "Thou believest that there is one God; thou doest well," the apostle James wrote. *"The devils also believe, and tremble"* (2:19).

The Soul Hustlers

Through his association with God before his fall, Satan is well aware of His majesty and omnipotence. Even though he was cast out of heaven, the faith Satan once had in his Creator as well as the knowledge he once professed are still noticeable in his communications to his earthbound agents. His nature, however, has transformed considerably since he first instigated revolt against the law of God, and the PSE findings fully embrace the validity of Christ's words found in John 8:43,44.

"Why do ye not understand my speech? even because ye cannot hear my words," Jesus admonished the Jews assembled at the temple.

"Ye are of your father the devil, and the lusts of your father ye will do. He was a murderer from the beginning, and *abode not in the truth, because there is no truth in him. When he speaketh a lie, he speaketh of his own: for he is a liar, and the father of it.*"

King Solomon said in Proverbs 12:22, "Lying lips are abomination to the Lord: but they that deal truly are his delight."

Christ could have been addressing today's psychic manipulators instead of the Jews, for thanks to the impartiality of the electron, we can now couple modern science to God's Word and observe His devastating judgment.

Notes

[1]Eileen Garrett, *Many Voices: The Autobiography of a Medium* (New York: G. P. Putnam's Sons, 1968), pp. 91ff.

[2]Allen Spraggett and William V. Rauscher, *Arthur Ford: The Man Who Talked With the Dead* (New York: W. W. Norton & Co., 1973), p. 71.

Will the Real Jeane Dixon Please Stand Up?

5

Will the Real Jeane Dixon Please Stand Up?

OF ALL THE LEADING PSYCHIC PROG-
nosticators, none has created as much controversy in my personal interview files and
PSE records as Jeane Dixon, the seer who has
never missed when foretelling assassinations . . .

Over the years — in fact, since the 1940s when she first
entered the Washington scene — she has been the subject of
an endless number of magazine and newspaper articles.
Books have been written about her, millions of Americans
read her astrology column in more than three hundred daily
newspapers, and those who do not follow her columns undoubtedly have read numerous predictions by her at one
time or another.

Among today's psychics, she is a superstar without
equal. The widely respected *Christian Herald* called her "the
nearest thing to an authentic . . . Old Testament prophet our
generation . . . is likely to see." H. L. Hunt, the late multimil-
lionaire, once called her "a prophet without equal among her
contemporaries."

The Soul Hustlers

I worked with Jeane Dixon for nearly a year in the preparation of the biography *Jeane Dixon – My Life and Prophecies*. If ever there was a woman breathing poise, eloquence, personality, charm, and a conviction that she has been chosen by God for a special role, it is Jeane Dixon.

Perhaps she has a right to feel this way, for none of her contemporary psychics can or dares to claim to have forecast so many untimely deaths as Jeane Dixon. She foretold the deaths of Carole Lombard and Marilyn Monroe; the tragic accident of Dag Hammarskjold of the United Nations; the assassinations of Mahatma Gandhi, President John F. Kennedy, Robert F. Kennedy, Martin Luther King, Jr., and others. Some have labeled her a prophet of doom, gloom, and damnation sparked occasionally by extreme right-wing politics. She has her share of loyal devotees, but equally as many watch her performances from the sidelines with rabid criticism and open scorn.

Without my divulging the outcome of the PSE evaluation at this point, let us examine this twentieth-century prophetic phenomenon and see *who* she really is; *why* she is; take a scrutinizing look at her predictions and Prophetic Accuracy Quotient. Let's compare personal experience with accounts published by respected journalists and see whether she really is the "prophet" she claims to be. Repeatedly she informed me that "the same spirit that worked through Isaiah and John the Baptist also works through me." Does she actually meet all the moral and biblical qualifications required of God's own prophets?

It was for a magazine assignment that I first became acquainted with Jeane Dixon. Unfamiliar with the vast realm of psychic phenomena, I meticulously dissected her unusual gift and wrote the story. It was a routine feature written without prejudice and based on my observations of her psychic track record. She was extraordinary — there was little doubt about that — and Clarence Dykeman, the man who first introduced me to her, was justified in describing "Mrs. D" as "nothing short of unbelievable."

Will the Real Jeane Dixon Please Stand Up?

Basically the "Jeane Dixon story" is a simple one, and her official biography is no more remarkable than that of many other well-known personalities.

Born Jeane Pinckert in a Wisconsin lumbering village shortly before the end of World War I, she left with her family at an early age for the Far West. As the child of Emma von Graffee and Frank Pinckert, she exhibited no unique character traits making her different from any other child. Her psychic ability — if it existed at that time — was certainly hidden.

At age forty-five, the story goes, Frank Pinckert moved his family to Santa Rosa, California. It was there that Jeane Pinckert's psychic abilities emerged for the first time in her eventful career. Upon learning one day that a gypsy woman had parked her wagon at a nearby estate, Jeane's mother decided to visit her, thereby exposing Jeane to another facet of life.

"The gypsy lady had a covered wagon with a stovepipe jutting out of the canvas roof," Jeane says. "Chickens poked their heads out of the wagon door, and a horse that was tied to a tree kicked and bounced wildly while we were there."[1] The official story continues by telling us that the gray-haired, old gypsy was forecasting a woman's fortune with cards as the Pinckerts arrived. But when Jeane's turn came and the woman held the child's hand in hers, something happened — and Jeane today is still filled with the mystery of it all.

"In fascination she pointed to the inside of my right hand," she remembers, "and exclaimed, 'She's got the Star of David in her hand, and here' — she gasped and took a second look — 'here's the Half Moon!' My mother smiled understandingly, for somehow she seemed to sense the significance of it all.

"The gypsy woman continued, 'Your child, madam, is destined for great things. In both her hands she has all the markings of a great mystic.'

"Lost in deep thought, she turned around and disappeared into her wagon. When she returned she had a ball in her hand — a crystal ball.

" 'Here, my little one,' she said softly, placing the ball gently into my outstretched hands. 'Take it — and tell me what you see.'

"I looked into it and what I saw was so beautiful it almost made me cry. I saw a wild rocky coast in a far-off land and a turbulent sea crashing into the jagged edges of the crumbling rocks. Giant waves split into a shower of tiny droplets of white foamy rain, drifting down and up again, losing themselves on the whisper of the wind. Farther inland, a sea gull aimed for the clouds, flying to fulfillment of his destiny.

" 'You are describing my homeland, little one,' the gypsy said sadly. 'You have just seen the most wonderful sights on earth. Keep the ball. It is yours. It can do more in your hands than in mine!' "[2]

"It was my first encounter with a gypsy," Jeane Dixon confessed in later years, "and *through that experience I began to realize that I had a specific purpose in life*" (emphasis added).

Jeane's reaction to this meeting was one of awe. I recall her telling me that her mother felt that if this was the Gift she was destined to possess, she prayed that her daughter would use it wisely. Mrs. Pinckert, however, did encourage Jeane to develop her "sixth" sense.

From published accounts we know that Jeane Pinckert's family moved to Los Angeles when she was a mere nine years old. There Jeane "read" for a woman who introduced herself as Marie Dressler. Dissatisfied with her faltering career in acting, Ms. Dressler opened a boarding house, but Jeane's "insight" into her future encouraged her to continue her acting career nevertheless. Today the success of Marie Dressler is history.

Another prediction Jeane proudly recollects involved Carole Lombard, the wife of Clark Gable. While in Bud Westmore's Beauty Salon an operator introduced Jeane to Miss Lombard, and when Jeane reached out her hand and touched Carole's, she felt a warming vibration.

Frightened by this sudden sensation, Jeane blurted,

Will the Real Jeane Dixon Please Stand Up?

"Oh, Miss Lombard, you must not go anywhere by plane for the next six months!"

A few days later the famous screen star died in a fiery plane crash.

Judging from the account in *A Gift of Prophecy* — proof-read and *approved* by Mrs. Dixon — we know that her marriage to James L. Dixon took place in the early 1940s, shortly after the war in Europe had begun. The resulting fever that gripped the United States just prior to its entry into the conflict soon enveloped James Dixon, and he joined the U.S. military effort as a dollar-a-year man, handling real estate acquisitions for the War Department.

This change in activity meant a swift move to Washington, D.C., and it was there that the Dixons grew to prominence. As a member of the Home Hospitality Committee, Jeane embarked on a new venture — "reading" the future for servicemen from adjacent hospitals and convalescent homes. Forecasting happiness and fame in a worrying nation is always an attention-getting occupation, and she was highly successful.

Though the war contributed to Jeane's initial recognition, it was not until many years after the conflict that it blossomed into fame. She became the most famous psychic of the postwar period. Nevertheless, while the war was still raging, she informed Harry S. Truman nonchalantly — when touching his fingertips at a party — that he would become President of the United States through an "act of God." She told Eric Johnson, former president of the National Chamber of Commerce, that he would soon occupy a high position in the motion picture industry; not long afterward, he became president of the Motion Picture Association of America. Also according to her recollections, she was invited to the White House at the request of President Franklin D. Roosevelt.

Describing that meeting with FDR, she said, "President Roosevelt, looking up from his desk, half raised his torso by his massive arms, flashed a warm smile, and said, 'Good morning, Jeane. Thank you for coming.' Wheeling himself toward the end of his desk, he shook her hand, and as he did so Jeane could almost feel the weight of the world pressing down on his broad shoulders.

"She took a chair at the corner of his desk, and they made small talk about the weather. Jeane, feeling a 'wave of loneliness reaching out toward her' finally said, 'Mr. President, it is wise to seek guidance sometimes, when one has a question in mind.'

"Roosevelt sighed as he responded, 'One's time is short, even at its longest. How much time do I have to finish the work I have to do?'

"'May I touch your fingertips?' she asked. He thrust forward his big hand, and as she picked up his vibrations, she sought desperately to divert the conversation and avoid an answer. When he insisted on a direct reply, she said reluctantly, 'Six months or less.' "[3]

Jeane commenced to forecast the loss of China to the Communists, a future alliance of the United States and Russia against Red China and the division of Germany into an Eastern and Western zone. Twice she met the president, according to her biographical information — once in November 1944, the second time in January 1945 — and both times in an advisory capacity.

Not until the publication of the book *A Gift of Prophecy* in August 1965 did Jeane really hit the big time. Looking for a best-selling subject, Washington political columnist Ruth Montgomery (at that time totally devoid of all psychic ability, yet now a renowned psychic medium) covered all the highpoints of Jeane's career, carefully sidestepping those unfulfilled prophecies that might raise eyebrows. The book made it big. More than three million copies have been sold thus far, and it still may be found on many paperback racks.

Jeane was accorded still more recognition in September 1969, when my biography, entitled *Jeane Dixon – My Life and Prophecies* appeared. With more than one million copies in print to date, that too made the national best-seller lists.

Anyone who has ever met Jeane Dixon will agree that she

is a very poised and fascinating woman. But this has not shielded her from becoming the subject of many controversies — one of which involves her Children to Children Foundation, an organization designed to improve the plight of children everywhere. Her role in the James L. Dixon real estate company is legendary, for her uncanny business talent is greatly praised (and feared) in the nation's capital.

On the surface, quite a woman.

To the undiscerning impartial observer, a success story.

But is this really all there is to Jeane Dixon?

Remember the tests of true prophets? Let's apply them to Jeane Dixon and see if this modern prognosticator is one of "God's very own."

Jeremiah 28:1 gave us the first test which states that the words of a true prophet must be fulfilled 100 percent. We do not have to probe too deeply to drive home the point that this qualification does not correspond with Mrs. Dixon's performance. Dr. Riesenman, the afore-mentioned parapsychologist in Arlington, Virginia, places her accuracy far below 80 percent; others rank her "God-given" ability as low as 16 percent. But perhaps we should let the prophet speak for herself.

In 1970 she predicted:

• Martha Mitchell will stay in the background and obey her husband.

• A Black Panther leader will be exposed to be paid by Moscow.

• A foreign source will reveal new facts about the death of President Kennedy before the middle of the year.

• Fidel Castro will lose his ruling position in Cuba and will physically be removed from his Caribbean island.

• Prime Minister Pierre Trudeau will not get married in the near future.

• August will be the month when there will be attempts on the life of President Nixon.

In 1971 she predicted:

• President Anwar Sadat of Egypt will not last.

- Johnny Cash will disappear rather mysteriously for a few months during the beginning of the year.
- King Hussein of Jordan will lose his throne.

She also forecast that Jacqueline Kennedy would not marry in 1968, but while her column carrying this announcement was still fresh, Mrs. Kennedy was marrying Aristotle Onassis on the island of Skorpios in the Aegean. A few years prior to that she predicted a presidential campaign for union leader Walter Reuther in 1964 and the end of the Vietnamese war in 1966.

But there's more. Nixon would not resign, according to Jeane Dixon, but her forecast was still wet ink when President Nixon vacated the White House. *My Life and Prophecies* was to sell almost as many copies as the Bible, she said. The Jeane Dixon Children to Children Hospital would soon be built, etc. etc. — all predictions that would have made captivating headlines if fulfilled, yet all failed! Surely Mrs. Dixon does not meet this first all-important qualification.

Does she prophesy in the name of the Lord? A conscientious appraisal of her prophetic pronouncements does not indicate this at all. "I predict," "I feel," "the vibrations I receive," "my vision," and other declarative phrases do not suggest a godly involvement. The third test too — that of not giving a private interpretation of prophecy — is grossly violated by America's best-known psychic.

At 7:17 A.M. on 5 February 1962, Jeane Dixon received one of her most memorable visions. She has described it thus:

"A child, born somewhere in the Middle East shortly after 7 a.m. (EST) on Feb. 5, 1962 will revolutionize the world. Before the close of the century he will bring together all mankind in one all-embracing faith. This will be the foundation of a *new Christianity*, with every sect and creed united through this man who will walk among the people to spread the wisdom of the Almighty Power. . . . He is the answer to the prayers of a troubled world."[4]

I know of Mrs. Dixon's belief in a conditional reincarnation. The child has to be a reincarnation of Christ — Christ reborn, in a new earthly body — a concept that is antibiblical and purely pagan. For several years Jeane continued to advocate that this Christ-child would guide the world in the early 1980s. The child was godly, he was divine, and he would become the salvation of the world.

Suddenly something happened.

While interviewing "Mrs. D" for *My Life and Prophecies*, I became aware of the inconsistencies in the revelation. Oversensitive to criticism, Mrs. Dixon soon changed her interpretation. "There is no doubt that he will fuse multitudes into one all-embracing doctrine," she explained in her "revised version." She continued, "He will form a new 'Christianity' based on his 'almighty power,' *but leading man in a direction far removed from the teachings and life of Christ, the Son.*"[5] Enlarging on her new interpretation, she called the child the "Antichrist" — a far cry from her first prophetic evaluation.

Another memorable interpretation that even managed to capture the newspaper headlines came as the result of a vision Mrs. Dixon experienced shortly after midnight, 14 July 1952. In this vision, a serpent crawled into her bedroom, slithered across the floor, and promised her all the wisdom of the ages if she'd only follow him. . . .

"Just imagine – Christ appeared to me in the form of a serpent, and will give me all the wisdom of the ages if I'd only follow him," she cried out triumphantly, when telling me her first interpretation of this vision.

But because of the counsel given by Father Kavan, a Jesuit scholar and trusted friend of Mrs. Dixon, and my research for the newly developing manuscript, she accepted the fact that Christ had never revealed Himself in the form of a serpent. Her acknowledgment of this was recorded in *My Life and Prophecies*.

"Thus, the first and most important part of my vision of the serpent was clarified," she said on page 174 of the second biography. "There was no doubt that the scholars were right when they asserted that 'the serpent among Christians is nothing else than the symbol of Satan, whose head will be crushed by the Son of Man when He comes.' . . . For the Christian, the serpent, the dragon of the Bible, is linked directly with the figure of the Antichrist."[6] No apology or explanation was given for her new interpretation.

Years later (1973), she lost a court case on just that vision. Accused of dishonesty in her dealings with Adele Fletcher, a well-known ghost writer, Mrs. Dixon was found guilty and was instructed to pay 5 percent of her share of the royalties of *My Life and Prophecies* when Miss Fletcher's attorney, Hubert M. Schlosberg, closed his summation by saying that anyone who couldn't make the distinction between a messenger of the devil and a messenger from God "cannot know the difference between right and wrong . . . in personal affairs."

"She has tried to use God as she has tried to use people," Schlosberg harshly concluded, "for her own financial gains. That is the only thing that means anything to Jeane Dixon."

A condemning statement indeed, but it is understandable how this impression is conveyed when interpretations of "godly visions" are changed to suit the readers.

Jeane Dixon also definitely does not "warn the people of God's coming judgment" in the biblical sense of the word. As for "recognizing a true prophet by the results of his work," the Adele Fletcher case casts serious doubts on Jeane's qualifications. And the divinity of Christ is openly questioned by her, since she believes in reincarnation and the multipurpose recycling of a soul. As to whether her predictions harmonize with biblical prophecies — well, that too leaves much to be desired.

James Bjornstad, author of the paperback *Twentieth Century Prophecy* — a small yet powerful book dealing with prophetic phenomena as manifested by Edgar Cayce and Jeane Dixon — says this of her:

"In conclusion, when one examines the multifarious elements involved in Biblical prophecy, one finds Jeane Dixon coming short of the standard set by the Scriptures.

"Is Jeane Dixon a prophetess of God? She certainly is not

a prophetess by either the qualifications recorded in the Old Testament or the New Testament."[7]

But to cover *all* the supernatural elements that might enter the psychic thrust in later years, God, through His prophet Isaiah, also laid down a more general rule to be used for those phenomena not specifically singled out. *"To the law* and to the testimony: if they speak not according to this word, it is because there is no light in them" (Isa. 8:20).

We are all familiar with the Law and regard it as an unfailing guideline for moral living and honesty, but it is at this point that failures often surface.

In March 1970, Stephen A. Schwartz and Harvey Katz, two enterprising journalists of the *Washingtonian* magazine, reported the findings of an investigation that had lasted several months. Based on scores of authentic interviews and painstaking examination of Jeane Dixon's tax records, their articles entitled "Whispers from Heaven for $5.95 plus tax" and "This is No Way to Run a Charity" shocked the social circles of Washington. The *Washingtonian* is highly respected in the nation's capital, and when it cracked the myth of her prosperous foundation and her psychic work, it put the first blemish on the face of the country's greatest psychic. Prior to publication, Mrs. D requested a meeting with the magazine's editor and threatened to file a $125 million lawsuit if the stories were published. The stories *were* published — with no repercussions.

Having worked closely with her in the development of my book and in the affairs of her Children to Children Foundation, I have no desire to attack her personal integrity. But she *is* a public figure and *does* claim to have God's inspiration, and therefore she is a fair target for critique.

These are my feelings and also those of fellow journalists, especially Daniel St. Albin Greene, ace investigative reporter for the *National Observer*. Greene wrote in the *Observer*'s edition of 27 October 1973,

"To her believers, Jeane Dixon is a Twentieth Century Nostradamus who foretold the assassinations of the brothers

Kennedy and manifold other calamities. To the cynical and the disillusioned, she's a glorified fortune teller fobbing off reactionary pap as divination.

"Prophet? Psychic? Phony?

"For weeks I tried to find out which, if any, of these desinations fits America's most famous crystal-ball gazer," he continued. *"What gradually emerged was a portrait of neither saint nor charlatan, but of a beguiling enigma whose real identity has been absorbed in the myth she herself created."*

Some two years after Greene's article was published, the PSE displayed its penetrating power on the very questions Dan Greene posed to Mrs. Dixon — with intriguing results. When dealing with public figures, journalists find it has become necessary to tape-record every interview to avoid misquotations and as a protection to both the subject and the reporter. Interviews are seldom printed as recorded, but always written up only after a thorough evaluation of the answers. Yet now this process has become more refined and more reliable, thanks to the discriminating qualities of the Psychological Stress Evaluator.

Much of Mrs. Dixon's initial fame rests on her counseling sessions with President Roosevelt. It has awarded her a certain amount of prestige among psychic believers, for no other psychic can make such claims. It lends respectability, a necessary ingredient in this profession.

During the impartial investigation launched by the *National Observer*, the incident was thoroughly checked and discussed with surviving members of the Roosevelt family. The results widened the credibility gap of Mrs. Dixon, relegating her claims to either the realm of fantasy or visions. Appointment calendars were checked; diaries were examined; Grace Tully, the only surviving Roosevelt secretary, was interviewed, together with Anna Roosevelt Halsted, daughter of FDR and one of his closest confidants — but no evidence could be found to substantiate Jeane Dixon's purported visits. Only Elliot Roosevelt, one of the president's sons, had a vague recollection of something to do with Mrs.

Will the Real Jeane Dixon Please Stand Up?

Dixon. He recalls that the president once remarked that he had met Jeane Dixon at some unnamed White House function — but that was all.

Did he recall any official visits of Mrs. D to the White House, or even a quiet, unobtrusive little chat in the president's office?

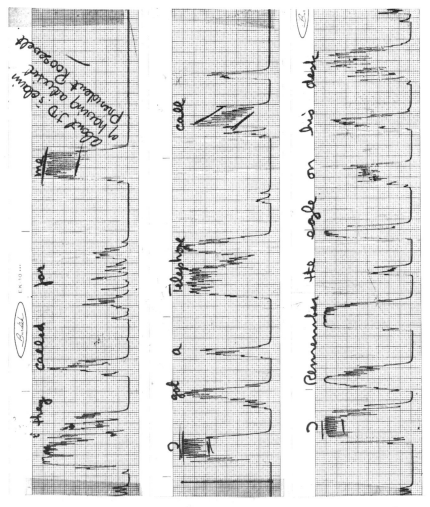

Figure 3. A PSE graph of a portion of Jeane Dixon's statements concerning a purported visit with President Franklin D. Roosevelt.

"Unless she appears on the records as a visitor," he told Dan Greene, "she was not invited to his office."

With permission of Daniel Greene, the tape-recorded interview in which Mrs. Dixon makes her White House claim was exposed to the PSE. The test tends to support the facts as uncovered by Greene's investigation.

Jeane Dixon's voice reveals the telltale points of stress usually associated with a conscious attempt to deceive. Pinpointing those areas that concern her so-called personal involvement, we note that the pronoun *me* in "they called for me"; the pronoun *I* in "I got a telephone call" (*call* also exhibited hard stress), and the *I* in "I remember the eagle on his desk" *were almost totally devoid of microtremors* (see figure 3). *Based on the norms used for PSE chart evaluation, I can reach no other conclusion but that Mrs. Dixon did not visit President Roosevelt at his invitation, nor did she receive a phone call inviting her, nor does she remember the "eagle on his desk."*

But this is only the tip of the proverbial iceberg, where Jeane Dixon is concerned.

The real controversies surrounding Jeane Dixon center on *her name; a missing period of fourteen years in her developing biography; a first marriage to a creamery plant foreman; her inability to remember exactly where she was born; where she attended school; where she was married to James L. Dixon and the wedding date of her second marriage, a union she still describes as her first marriage!*

To an investigative journalist, these questions are vitally important, considering the fact that the subject is someone in whom so many people put their unwavering trust. Either Mrs. Dixon's memory is fading into forgetfulness, in which case the results of the investigation should be welcomed by her, or other reasons have compelled her to create a new identity.

Which one of the two shall it be? Only Mrs. Dixon knows, but we do not stand here as her accusers, merely as an aid to her memory.

When speaking about prophets, we often picture in our

minds men of old walking the Judean desert, dressed in long burnooses, holding a shepherd's rod. For several years now, while lecturing on "psychics and prophets," I invariably draw comparisons with today's prognosticators who are attired in evening gowns and tuxedos . . . and now it seems the analogy is right. Jeane Dixon is not only the prophetic spearhead of the twentieth century, *she is also one of the oldest of today's prophets, if not the oldest!*

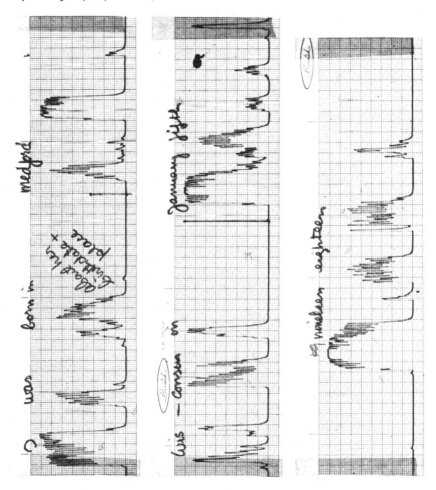

Figure 4. Jeane Dixon's statement about her birth.

The Soul Hustlers

When I wrote Jeane's biography six years ago, she told me that her age was "in the late forties"; let's say forty-eight. This happened in 1969, which means that in 1976, her age should be *fifty-five*. Her passport, however, gives her birthdate as 5 January 1918, making her *fifty-eight* in 1976. But that isn't all. When Adele Fletcher brought her breach-of-contract suit against Mrs. Dixon in 1973, in a pretrial deposition Jeane stated she was born on 5 January 1910, making her not *fifty-five*, not *fifty-eight*, but *sixty-six!* . . . and was highly indignant when a Washington-based journalist wrote a trial story about the "sixty-three-year-old prophet."

But there's more — the story of "Washington's own prophet" is a long one.

In the course of his investigation for the *National Observer*, Daniel Greene disclosed details of her life which had been concealed for many years, yet no one really knows why. The Pinckert family (Jeane's maiden name) consisted of, not seven children as mentioned in *A Gift of Prophecy*, but ten — nine of them born in Medford, Wisconsin, the youngest after the family moved to Missouri.

So what's the mystery?

It arises when trying to establish the correct birthdate, the birthplace, the ranking in the family's birth chronology (Jeane claims she is the youngest), and the elementary school she attended. These particulars Mrs. Dixon's memory no longer seems able to supply. A tape-recorded interview with Jeane tells us that "I was born in Medford, Wisconsin, on January fifth, nineteen-eighteen." When examined on the Psychological Stress Evaluator, this statement produces too many high and medium stress points to be believable (see figure 4). What's more, an in-the-field investigation substantiates this. A diligent and thorough search of the birth records of Medford, Wisconsin, for the year 1918, conducted by the *National Observer*, does not indicate that a Jeane Pinckert was born in that year. The youngest member of the family was born in Missouri following the Pinckerts' move from Wisconsin; consequently, *Jeane must have been born in*

Will the Real Jeane Dixon Please Stand Up?

Medford, but in a different year! The recorded answer is so stress-filled that the emotional strain of voicing it colored the entire sentence! Is it possible that at birth she was registered under a different name?

Reports the *National Observer*, "He [Frank Pinckert] and his German wife, Emma, produced not seven but 10 children. Birth records in Wisconsin indicate that the first nine were born between 1895 and 1910, in this order: Elsie, Erna, Walter, Ella, Curt, Lydia (originally recorded as "Lillie"), Erny, Evelyn and Victor." Jeane must have been one of these, but which one?

Interviews with surviving members of the family have supplied the only possible answer. All agree that Jeane Dixon is in reality Lydia Pinckert, born in January 1904, thereby making her not fifty-five, fifty-eight, sixty-six, but *seventy-two* years old. Feeding her recorded denials into the PSE, we again received confirmation of this report. The words "My name has been Jeane — Lydia isn't this girl" created sufficient stress to support the findings of the investigation.

Why this obvious discrepancy?

Granted, an aging woman celebrity might want to erase a span of fourteen years, but why go to such extremes?

Perhaps the answer can be found in Santa Ana, California, where in January 1928 a marriage certificate was filed for Charles Zuercher, a Swiss immigrant, and Jeane A. Pinckert, daughter of Frank and Emma Pinckert. According to the documents in the Santa Ana archives, the groom was thirty-seven at the time of the marriage, and the bride twenty-two. Zuercher can no longer be interviewed about his marriage, which ended in divorce: he died in November 1940.

Is this indeed Jeane Dixon's first husband, the one her sisters vaguely remember?

She definitely does not acknowledge a previous marriage, but both the research and the PSE indicate otherwise.

To my thinking, credibility is one of the greatest assets a person can have, and God's prophets certainly must be beyond reproach. Can it be perhaps that she entered the secular prophetic field with high ideals, but found her early life out of tune with her newly developed vocation?

This no one knows but Mrs. Dixon.

Besides violating God's tests of a true prophet, it is also evident now that she places more faith in astrology than the Bible. She says, "As a child I was taught Chaldean astrology by a wise and wonderful man . . . a Jesuit priest [Father Henry]. . . . I don't see how anyone can say that astrology is wrong. . . . After all, he was a man of God." And with this as basic philosophy, she presently has a daily astrology column reported to appear in three hundred newspapers, guiding millions of readers with principles gleaned from the Chaldeans.

Astrology is quite a business, but there was a time when Mrs. Dixon was merely a "seer," not an astrologer. How did she get involved with it? There are diverse theories, but the most plausible one is explained by Daniel Logan, a New York psychic.

"Frankly, I am getting a little fearful about these people who start as one thing and suddenly begin to be experts in totally new areas," Logan writes. "One of these people goes on a television show and a week later she is approached by four publishers, a business organization, an agent, a manager — I know I was, and I'm sure many others are. And the approaches are 'Gee, would you like to write an astrology column for a hundred thousand dollars a year, no questions asked?' If you reply, 'Oh, I don't know anything about astrology,' they tell you, 'That's all right, we'll just use your name and get someone to do the column.'

"Or you take Omar's from five years ago and just change the dates and rephrase a little. Which, in one well-known case, is true. The person had taken material five years old, written by somebody else, and simply altered a few words in each of the entries, and made a fortune.

"The money is very enticing."[8]

But Mrs. Dixon writes her own columns, you say; consequently this does not apply to her.

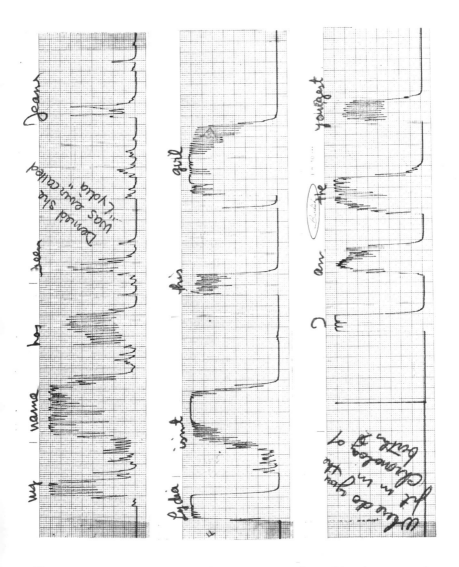

Figure 5. This and the following PSE graphs relate Jeane Dixon's statements regarding her birth and early life.

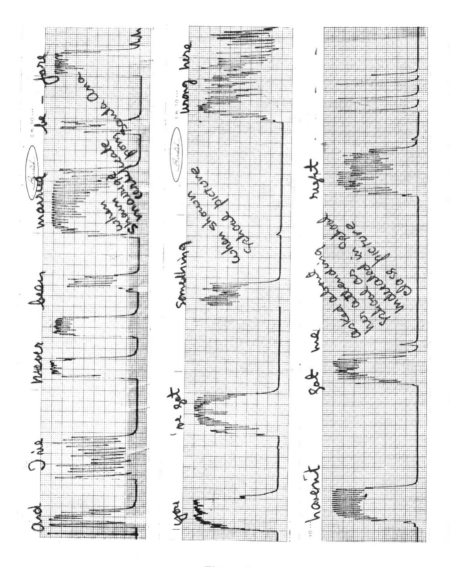

Figure 5a.

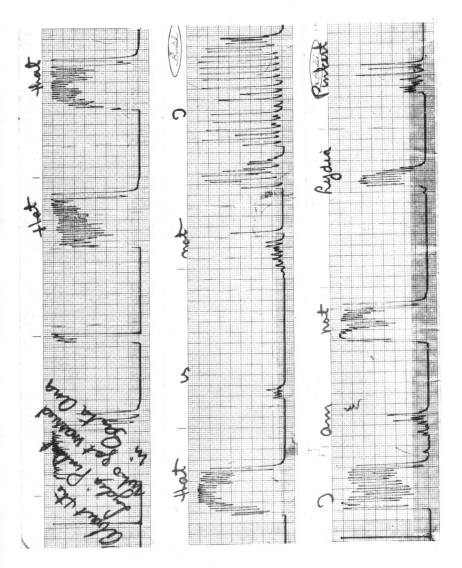

Figure 5b.

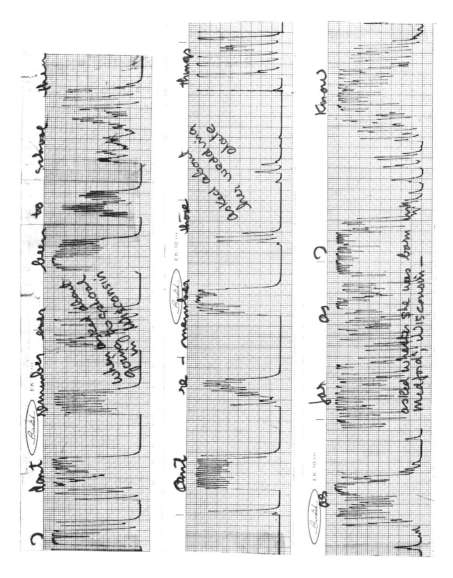

Figure 5c.

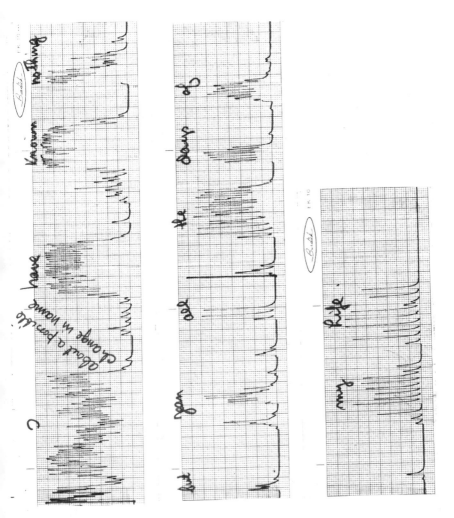

Figure 5d.

Will the Real Jeane Dixon Please Stand Up?

Jim Seymore also felt that way until the tracks of investigation led him to believe otherwise. Perhaps this is the reason why, when exposing the origin of Mrs. Dixon's column, he did not encounter any legal opposition or threats of lawsuits. Writing in the *Washingtonian* magazine, Seymore said pointedly,

"She [Mrs. Dixon] does not mention that the column is actually written in New York by the divorced wife of a former Dixon employee. When I questioned Robert Gillespie, who handles promotion of the Dixon Horoscope for the Chicago Tribune-New York Daily News Syndicate, about the woman, he replied, 'She's kept very much in the background. I doubt that she will speak to you.' "

Inquiries suggesting that anyone else is involved in producing her column are met with a stern denial from Jeane Dixon. "I write my own column," she reprimanded me tersely, when I questioned her concerning this report. "I do them late at night when no one else is around — so I can concentrate." Again — a blatant contradiction. But should she be telling the truth, then she is openly violating God's admonition to shun the practice of "observing times" (Deut. 18:10), and by doing so has ranked herself among those who are called "an abomination unto the Lord" (v. 12).

Who is Jeane Dixon, really?

The facts have emerged through long and painstaking investigations conducted by many reliable reporters, and the picture that surfaces is one of contradictions and misrepresentations.

Though Jeane Dixon does prophesy with a high percentage of accuracy, her work most definitely does not meet the qualifications required for a prophet of God — a "true prophet." She violates His rules. Her accuracy quotient is based on destructive and death-dealing prophecies, not on those that elevate the human mind and soul. Her personal life, which should be above reproach if she is a true prophet, is a conglamoration of contradictions, the truth of which can now be documented.

The Soul Hustlers

Is she a true prophet gone awry, or is she inspired by satanic forces?

My investigation compels me to accept the latter view, for no one who seeks after truth in the name of God can consciously violate His laws and hope to be excused.

Her phenomenon is not new. Christ foresaw its emergence almost two thousand years ago when he spoke about the endtime: "And many false prophets shall rise, and shall deceive many. . . . Then if any man shall say unto you, Lo, here is Christ, or there; believe it not. For there shall arise false Christs, and false prophets, and shall shew great signs and wonders; insomuch that, if it were possible, they shall deceive the very elect" (Matt. 24:11,23,24).

Anything we can say in conclusion about Mrs. Dixon's prophetic ability is decidedly superfluous.

Notes

[1]Ruth Montgomery, *A Gift of Prophecy* (New York: William Morrow & Co., 1965), p. 15.

[2]Rene Noorbergen, *Jeane Dixon – My Life and Prophecies* (New York: William Morrow & Co., 1969), pp. 53-54.

[3]Ruth Montgomery, *A Gift of Prophecy*, pp. 46-47.

[4]Ibid., p. 181.

[5]Rene Noorbergen, *Jeane Dixon – My Life and Prophecies*, p. 194.

[6]Ibid., p. 174.

[7]James Bjornstad, *Twentieth Century Prophecy* (New York: Pyramid Books, 1970), pp. 63-64.

[8]M. M. Delfano, *The Living Prophets* (New York: Dell Publishing Co., 1972), p. 161.

The Counterfeit

6

6   The Counterfeit

6 "YE MEN OF GALILEE, WHY STAND YE gazing up into heaven? this same Jesus, which is taken up from you into heaven, *shall so come in like manner as ye have seen him go into heaven"* (Acts 1:11).

Something strange is in the making for humanity; that is, if we are prepared to believe the utterings of the psychic masters of today. For as time slips slowly by, new and urgent predictions about an imminent celestial event have managed to seep into their forecasts, and the psychic survey has once again found evidence of this persistent development.

The psychics have done their job amazingly well. Not only do 53 percent of all Americans now believe in their work, but almost as an afterthought, four out of every ten Americans currently believe in flying saucers, or UFOs as they are commonly called. Thousands of unexplainable sightings, both here and abroad, have given rise to the wildest rumors, often adding to the increasing uncertainty in the minds of men. The psychics have taken advantage of this flying-saucer neurosis by reinforcing the already confused situation with their supernaturally supplied UFO impressions.

The UFO survey discovered that specific regions of the United States react differently to the UFO craze, as do psychic believers. In the western part of the country, for example, 53 percent are UFO believers, while the Bible-belt south has only 31 of every 100 believing in the unknown phenomena. It also shows that a full 48 percent of all the white-collar workers back their existence, and those in the 18-29 age bracket are more convinced than their elders.

Again, something strange is happening. Both psychic belief and faith in the UFOs are on the increase. Is there possibly a connection between the two? Can it be that the 40 percent who believe in UFOs are part of the 53 percent who believe in the occult?

This question has not been investigated by any survey thus far, but in my work with practitioners and believers in the psychic world, I have yet to encounter an individual whose faith in the supernormal is not reinforced by a belief in unidentified flying objects. They complement one another.

It was my recent survey interview with the West Coast psychic George King that directed my attention to this topic. King has resided in my files since our first interview nearly twenty years ago in a London suburb where he lived at the time; aware of his intense involvement in the supernatural, I considered it a "must" to include him in the Soul Hustlers Survey.

King's psychic credentials are impressive. He is the president of an organization known as the Aetherius Society, a flying-saucer-oriented cult based on supernormal revelations. He is a spiritual healer, a psychic, a clairvoyant, a medium, and a psychometrist, and he controls a tightly knit group of disciples whose lives are guided by his spiritual counsel.

In checking his beliefs on the survey form and comparing them with other psychics who have an unshakable trust

The Counterfeit

in UFOs, I find a thread of decidedly anti-Christian convictions, binding them together in an unbreakable bond.

Why discuss UFOs in this book? Is it relevant, or is there merely a superficial connection? And if there is — what can be its true significance?

It was for *Vizier*, a Dutch illustrated magazine, that I first visited George King, self-styled Ambassador for Interplanetary Parliament and Primary Terrestrial Channel Number One. A mystery — that's what his neighbors used to call him; to them, this designation was more than justifiable.

It was 1959, and postwar England was caught up in fresh industrial development. Business boomed everywhere. Piccadilly Circus was once again the focal point of teenage exuberance. Expense-account-heavy executives roamed the streets of Soho, and happy laughter filled the subways at rush hour. London had survived not only the war, but its convulsive reconstructive period as well; it showed in the prosperous and carefree attitude of its citizenry.

But on the fringes of the city, a strange phenomenon was taking place. George King told me the story in his London apartment at our first encounter:

"It began back in '54 when a bodiless voice first spoke to me in a soft, quiet, yet melodious way," George said gently. "'Be prepared to become the Voice of Interplanetary Parliament,' the voice stated, . . . and from that time on I have had to act as Primary Terrestrial Channel Number One. Ever since that moment, I receive strange impulses from the vast regions beyond the earth informing me when 'they' will transmit through me — "

"Who are these 'they' you talk about?" I interrupted George. "What do they tell you?"

He was silent for a moment. Then his eyes scanned my face, and he answered, "The beings I am in contact with have identified themselves as Mars Sector Six, Mars Sector Eight, the Master Aetherius, and others. They usually begin their transmission to me with their name identification. They are known to me as the 'Cosmic Masters.' They represent Interplanetary Parliament on Venus and are superintelligent. They contact me from their flying saucers, with which they constantly roam about the earth — "

"Why *you*, George, why you?"

George King stood up and walked around his small living room. He gestured excitedly.

"They have chosen me because of my deep knowledge of cosmic matters and my devoted interest in metaphysics," he replied carefully, as if weighing every word for its effect. "They counsel and prophesy, and the frightening thing is that their predictions and warnings have come true innumerable times."

He leaned over and flipped on the switch of a nearby tape recorder, thus introducing me to MARS SECTOR SIX — a terrifying voice full of doom and damnation. It was just a few words, but intriguing enough for us to decide to watch George King experience a transmission planned for later that day.

My diary for that night tells it all.

"It is now seven o'clock. . . . I am sitting in the living room of the home of George King," I whispered into the Miniphone wire recorder. "Brightly burning fireplace . . . it's raining outside . . . typical London evening. Members of George's group are sitting across from us, watching George with the same intensity as we are . . . waiting for his contact.

"George is slowly scanning the people . . . his eyes are closing . . . his breathing becomes shallow . . . slower and slower. Nervously the muscles in his face contract . . . he shivers . . . a deep sigh . . . Grace [his secretary] switches on the tape recorder . . . he sighs again . . . very deeply this time . . . *there's the voice* . . . I recognize it!"

An unearthly sound, heavy as a clap of rolling thunder, booms through the mouth of the entranced George King, telepathic medium of the Cosmic Masters.

> THIS IS MARS SECTOR EIGHT . . . GENERAL MESSAGE . . .

There is a short but pregnant pause, then the voice is heard again.

The Counterfeit

WE WARN ALL EARTH SCIENTISTS THAT THE CONTINUATION OF
THE PRESENT ATOMIC EXPERIMENTS MAY CAUSE A SHIFT IN THE
MOUNTAINS OF THE BOTTOM OF THE OCEAN . . . IF THIS HAPPENS,
AND THIS WILL HAPPEN IF YOU CONTINUE YOUR IDIOTIC EXPERI-
MENTS, THEN IT WILL HAVE ITS REPERCUSSIONS ON EARTH FOR
MANY CENTURIES TO COME . . .

"The voice has died out," my diary continues, "but not for
long. It returns, but now, thin and shrill, high-pitched, completely different from the one that started the transmission."

NEVER BEFORE HAVE I CALLED TERRA . . . I, FROM THE PLANET
NEPTUNE, AM CIRCLING YOUR GLOBE . . . WE HAVE DISCOVERED
THAT YOU ARE 493 OUT OF YOUR REGULAR ORBIT . . . THIS ABERRA-
TION HAS MOVED THE EARTH'S MAGNETIC FIELD AND WILL HAVE
METEOROLOGICAL RESULTS OVER THE ENTIRE GLOBE . . . THE ELEC-
TROMAGNETIC FIELD OF EARTH IS IN DANGER OF GETTING OUT OF
BALANCE . . . AND IF MARS HAD NOT ALREADY PROJECTED AN
IMPORTANT SYSTEM OF FORCELINES ON TERRA VIA THE MOON, THE
MOVEMENT OF TERRA AROUND ITS AXIS WOULD HAVE CHANGED
COMPLETELY . . . THIS WOULD HAVE MEANT A TERRIBLE CATAS-
TROPHE AS IN THAT CASE 75 PERCENT OF THE EARTH'S WATER
WOULD HAVE COME INTO MOTION . . . THE DELUGE WILL COME
AGAIN, ON TERRA, BUT THIS TIME MORE TERRIBLE THAN DURING
THE TIME OF ATLANTIS . . . IF CONTINUATION OF YOUR ATOMIC
RESEARCH IS WORTH THIS RESULT, THEN GO ON THIS ROAD TO
TOTAL DESTRUCTION OF YOUR PLANET . . . ALL RESPONSIBILITY
RESTS ON YOU . . .

"Neptune stops as suddenly as he had begun," my diary
reads, "and now the sinister voice of MARS SECTOR EIGHT takes
over, still sounding as cold and menacing as before."

OF COURSE YOU ARE FREE TO . . . AS USUAL . . . TO DISREGARD
THIS WARNING, the voice rasps through the otherwise si-
lent room, BUT THERE IS NO MARGIN FOR ERRORS . . . STOP HERE
OR BE DESTROYED . . . IF NOT . . . THAT MAN MAY BE MERCIFUL UNTO
ONE ANOTHER . . . THIS IS MARS SECTOR EIGHT . . . AN EMERGENCY
TRANSMISSION . . .

"George King's voice changes to an indistinct mumbling sound. The transmission is finished. We look at George. No longer is he the strong vibrant man of an hour ago. He seems completely drained and exhausted. He relaxes for a few moments . . . now his natural color is returning to his face . . . he gets up and stumbles out of the room . . . "

I turned off the Miniphone.

Later that same evening, I had a long discussion with King, and he filled me in on the more phenomenal aspects of his supernatural contacts.

"They forecast through me when their flying saucers can be seen," King confessed with discernible pride. "And where! For example, 1957 was a busy year in this respect. I vividly remember the transmission made through me on the nineteenth of May, when my contact told us that we would be able to see their spaceships on Monday the twentieth, right here over London. That same night several people did see bright yellow moving lights hang over the city. Needles of golden light appeared in the darkened evening sky. No planes were over the city at that time, and many people stood aghast, staring at the sky — "

"But there's more to it than just forecasting the appearances of their spaceships?"

"In January 1957, the MASTER AETHERIUS declared,

ON MANY PLACES VISIONS WILL BE SEEN OF THE MASTER JESUS AND OF THE WOMAN WHO IS COMMONLY KNOWN AS HIS MOTHER . . .

The fulfillment of this was printed in the London *Evening News* of 11 September 1957, when the Associated Press released the following news item. George picked up a folder and read,

WARSCHAU — In Krakau, the appearance of the Virgin Mary has created great disturbance among civic and church authorities. For the last two weeks, every evening a large number of people gathered in front of the house where Miss Cseslawa Janusz, 49, has seen the vision of the Virgin Mary for two times. The crowd sings spiritual songs hoping that she will also appear to them. The Polish Catholic newspaper Tygwonik Powzsechny has warned against hysteria.

Repeatedly King's "contacts" forecast the appearances of UFOs, and nearly every time sightings were reported in major newspapers.

That was in 1959, and flying saucers were at that time a rather new development. However, predicting their presence in combination with prophecy was news and helped catapult the UFO craze to where it is today.

Things have a way of changing. In my latest interview with George King, his answers were polished and carefully guarded, undoubtedly the result of nearly twenty years of critical newspaper exposure. Even though his contacts with the Cosmic Masters are still as real as ever to him — his news releases and magazine *Cosmic Masters* testify to that — his religious philosophy has solidified into something more tangible, with decidedly anti-Christian views.

"The devil, sir, is dead!" King declared unhesitatingly when I asked him whether he believed the devil to be an evil being (see figure 6). "He was indeed an evil being, but is no longer. He was active until a few years ago, when he was transmuted into another body! He no longer exists."

King also does not believe in the actual second coming of Christ, but rather claims that *Christ first came to us in a UFO and that His return as a "cosmic master" will also be via UFO!*

In checking my files on material supplied to me by King in years past, I found doctrinal substance dictated to him by his cosmic masters — all unequivocally anti-Christian. Listen to the MASTER AETHERIUS:

THE MASTER JESUS WAS RESIDENT ON VENUS[1] . . . WHEN THE PERSON CALLED JESUS CAME TO THIS PLANET FROM VENUS . . . [2]

THE EVOLUTION OF MANKIND IS NOW BEING SPEEDED UP, IN ORDER TO REACH A CERTAIN TIME LIMIT . . . COOPERATE WITH THE SPEEDING UP, HELP IT, BECOME THE BEINGS WHO SPEED THIS UP, AND I PROMISE YOU A MILLION HELPERS . . . [3]

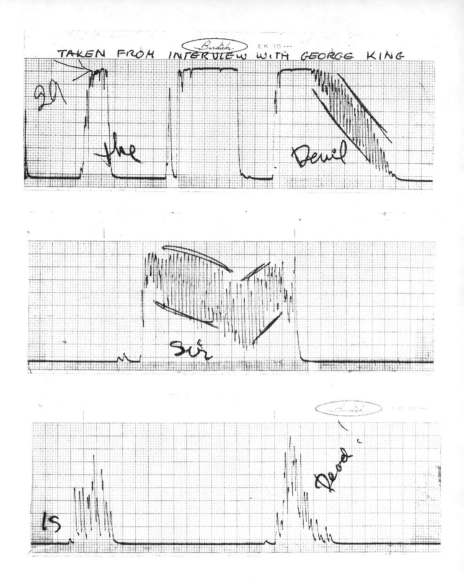

Figure 6. The *hard stress* on these graphs is too severe to be ignored. The Devil is not dead by any means — and George King knows it!

But there's more. The same "cosmic master" dictates,

> THE TIME WILL HAVE TO COME WHEN THE WESTERN RELIGIOUS
> LEADERS AND TEACHERS WILL HAVE TO TAKE FROM ORIENTAL
> TEACHERS CERTAIN THINGS WHICH ARE ACCEPTABLE TO THEM AND

The Counterfeit

PUT THEM INTO PRACTICE . . . SO OUR MESSAGE TO YOUR RELIGIOUS
LEADERS THROUGHOUT THE WESTERN WORLD IS TO BE PREPARED
TO INTRODUCE INTO YOUR TEACHINGS, TRUTHS ABOUT REINCAR-
NATION, SO THAT YOU CAN GIVE YOUR FOLLOWERS A BETTER,
TRUER, AND MORE UNDERSTANDABLE PICTURE OF THE LAW WHICH
IS GOD . . . [4]

THE TIME HAS COME WHEN CERTAIN CHERISHED FOUNDATIONS
MUST BE TORN UP BY THE ROOTS AND CAST ONTO THE FIRE OF
DISCRIMINATING TRUTHS TO BE TRANSMUTED . . . THE RELIGIOUS
LEADERS OF TERRA HAVE THIS RESPONSIBILITY IN THE COMING AGE
. . . YOUR BIBLE HAS TO BE REWRITTEN . . . IT HAS TO CONTAIN MORE
OF THE TRUTH IN A MORE UNDERSTANDABLE WAY THAN IT DOES AT
PRESENT . . . [5]

As of late, the contacts of George King with the beings from
the outer regions have undergone significant modifications.
His dialogue is no longer limited to conversations with the
cosmic masters known to him since the early 1950s. In fact,
before his departure from England another voice was added
to the increasing number of unearthly contacts.

Recently I had an opportunity to compare the latest recorded release of that voice with recordings I made while still
in London. The voice is the same — no doubt about that —
but so is the intensity and its gentle velvet timbre, full of
compassionate love . . . a soft, sweet baritone voice, filled
with concern for the human race.

I listened to it and felt a tingling shiver of fear race down
my spine. I flipped the switch and listened once more. There
it was in all its fullness.

*I am Jesus, who stepped upon this world to bring the way to
God through love and service,* the satiny voice caressed. *I now
bless those who give service to their brothers and to God in this
way.*

*Thrice blessed are the healers for they will bring light into my
church. For they are the ones who – when the time is ripe – will
lead my church.*

So ends the sixth blessing.

As I listened to the recording, my mind flashed back to a

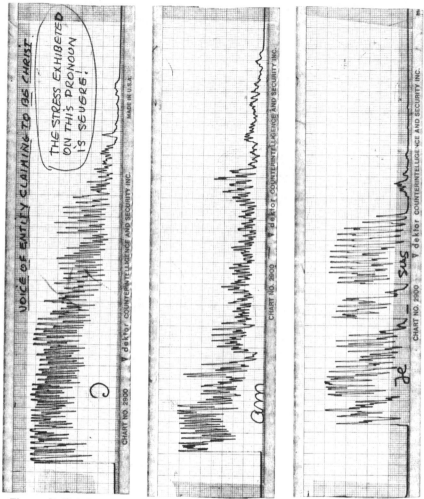

Figure 7. This is a voice speaking through George King and claiming to be Jesus Christ.

familiar Bible text. "And no marvel," it reads in 2 Corinthians 11:14, "for Satan himself is transformed into an angel of light."

Could this possibly be *the* angel the Bible refers to?

The PSE is a marvelous invention, and moments after the voice first filled my office, its vibrations were exposed to the PSE's electronic circuitry. It was routine — yet different. This was not a man, George King, speaking with knowledge stored in his mind. True, the sound emanated from King, but only because the entity calling itself Jesus had decided to use King's voicebox. The PSE was not really evaluating the voice of King, it was testing the power that manipulated his voicebox. It was judging the honesty of the entity that controlled the medium.

Only three words were needed and it was all over.

The words "I am Jesus" examined by the PSE (figure 7) said it all. Tremendous emotional tension was evident. Because it was not originating from King — since he was in trance and devoid of all emotional stress — it could only be stress produced by an unmitigated attempt to deceive, coming from the entity that superimposed its will on the larynx of the psychic.

What does this all mean?

For some time now, prominent psychics and mediums in the United States and Great Britain have announced concise forecasts similar to those outlined by George King when he predicted that "a cosmic master" will come to earth in a flying saucer. They have predicted a close contact with the beings controlling the UFOs before the end of 1976.

Bernardine Villanueva, a former Florida model-turned-psychic and one who has an uncanny accuracy quotient when making predictions, said, "Within the next eighteen months we will see absolute conclusive proof of UFOs. Space beings will stay around to communicate with both press and television. They will stay long enough for people to actually learn about their existence and visit the UFOs, and will impart extremely valuable medical knowledge which will do away with many of our known diseases."[6]

Simon Alexander, well-known British psychic prophet, pointed out that "this meeting will become the greatest thing in the history of the human race." This feeling was echoed by both Shawn Robbins and Clara Schuff, psychics with a high degree of accuracy.

Even Sybil Leek, one of the foremost astrologers in the U.S., issued her own forecast on this subject, based of course on astrology. Ms. Leek said, "So many respectable citizens will come forward with startling information about their meetings with visitors from space that the U.S. military will officially admit these aliens have come to earth to observe us.

Olaf Johnson concurs in his most recent interview with me: "The contacts between them and us will be for the good of mankind."

Is it perhaps possible that meaningful contacts between "them" and "us" have already taken place?

There are those who firmly believe that this has indeed been the case. The flying saucer craze that followed the Second World War has spurred the publication of many books dealing with this subject. As of late this has taken on a new dimension — propagating the idea that beings from other planets have observed and visited us for thousands of years. Some writers and pseudoscientists have gone as far as suggesting that Latin America shows remains of ancient spaceports; that alien space beings have left tangible signs of their advanced civilization on various spots on this planet. Fascinating as this theory may be, it is totally unbiblical and certainly unacceptable from a purely scientific point of view.

The hard core evidence just isn't there.

Not all psychics openly declare that something supernatural is on the threshold of presenting itself to us in a physical way. In the survey, I directed the customary eighty-seven questions to the Memphis psychic, David Bubar. Nearly every answer I received I had anticipated; however, when questions 61, 63, and 65 were asked, his voice pattern revealed an unexpected reaction.

"Have we been visited by beings from other planets (UFOs)?" (61) I asked David, and the negative response that I recorded displayed so much intense emotional stress that I know it was either a conscious or a subconscious attempt to deceive (figure 8). Questions 63 and 65 — "Have you ever seen a UFO?" and "Did you receive psychic forecasts of appearances of UFOs?" — triggered a like reaction.

Are David and the other psychics hiding more from us

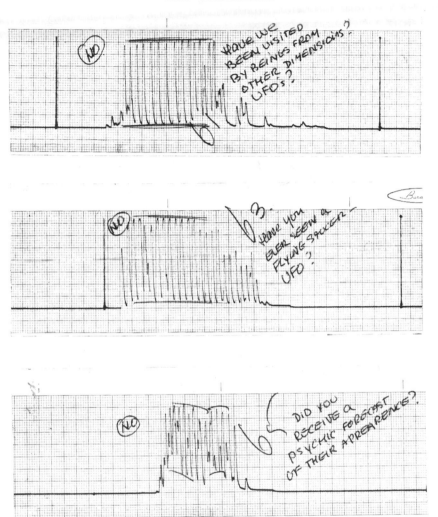

Figure 8. David Bubar's response.

than we think? Are we to believe that soon there will be an actual body-contact with beings from the UFOs, and that this first contact will be a prelude to the second coming of Christ via an unidentified flying object?

Christians simply cannot accept this!

The Bible is unmistakably clear on the point that Jesus'

return will be on the clouds of heaven "in like manner as ye have seen him go into heaven" (Acts 1:11). Are the psychics perhaps surreptitiously attempting to prepare us to accept a devilish counterfeit?

It is essential for us to remember that the devil knows and understands more about biblical prophecy than we do. He was a witness to events before the creation of man; he observed God guiding His prophets in charting the course of history long before the events took place; and he can certainly make a reasonably accurate guess as to how rapidly we are approaching the end of days. There is an end to God's patience, and Satan knows it!

The devil's time is running out.

"Woe to the inhabiters of the earth and of the sea! for the devil is come down unto you, having great wrath, because *he knoweth that he hath but a short time*" (Rev. 12:12).

"Be sober, be vigilant; because your adversary the devil, as a roaring lion, walketh about, seeking whom he may devour" (1 Peter 5:8).

Can we really expect a major satanic manifestation with a UFO as a vehicle?

A recent survey conducted among members of the French branch of Mensa International, a group of the world's most intelligent people elected to membership because of their high IQs, shows that 93 percent of them firmly believe in the existence of UFOs. Other figures tell us that a majority of the same people — precisely 52 out of 100 — have already endorsed the idea that these objects come from outer space, and not from our world. Still other polls — and there have been several over the past few years — indicate that more than 80 percent of all Americans who believe in the existence of UFOs support this outer space theory. What's more, they are convinced that the spaceships come from other planets in our solar system!

As a nation we are being habituated to the idea of a major UFO manifestation. Leading psychiatrists attest to this.

"I think the UFOs would be dealt with pretty realistically," finds Dr. Benjamin Simon of Boston. "I am sure there would be far less excitement than most people think. Most people have become so accustomed to the idea of UFOs and space travel, they would accept a UFO pretty easily today."

Dr. Harold Esler of Farmington, Michigan, substantially agrees with his Boston colleague. "Most people would react in relation to their own personalities," he reasons. "They would be stunned, but those who are kind and trusting would want to get involved with the flying saucer occupants and welcome them."

A third psychiatrist feels that it would be almost an everyday occurrence. Dr. Louis Rittlemayer of Washington, D.C., says, "There might be some initial panic among the people who first saw it, but not the rioting-in-the-streets kind of thing that science-fiction movies have portrayed. The reaction would be the same as to any other surprising, inconceivable event. It would be one of shock. And, if the UFO occupants were peaceful, maybe nothing more after the initial shock."[7]

During the past three years, the UFO sightings have become more realistic, more varied, and more daring in their appearances. In 1973, a four-man U.S. Army helicopter crew experienced a terrifying encounter with a UFO in the skies over eastern Ohio. In October 1974, two veteran troopers of the Pennsylvania State Police watched in shocked silence as a strange, heart-shaped UFO hovered as if suspended over a grove of trees near Middletown Township in Pennsylvania, painting the night scene with a beam of brilliant white light. Policemen in Tilton, New Hampshire, were frightened when a hovering, pulsating UFO chased their squad car.

Air Force pilots, airline pilots, sheriffs, and ordinary citizens continue to relate year after year the unusual happenings. Either the "spaceships" are now being seen more frequently, or the observers realize that they will no longer be regarded as mentally unstable and consequently have no qualms when talking about the sightings.

Thus hundreds of persons to this date have told of observing the eerie aerial displays — a phenomenon that defies all rational explanation. Yet, if such have been seen, they must originate from somewhere and be guided by something.

TABLE 4

Question	Correct psychic answers in percentages
Do you believe in spirit communication?	96
Do you believe in life during death?	100
Do you believe in the actual second coming of Christ?	24
Do you believe the devil is an evil being/power?	30
Is Christ a personal being?	8
Was Christ a superpsychic human being?	72
Do you believe in astrology?	88
Can a true psychic duplicate the wonders wrought by Christ?	84
Are the biblical prophecies dealing with the end of the world still valid?	24
Do you warn the people of God's coming judgment?	20
Are your predictions in absolute harmony with those of the biblical prophets?	20
Do you point out the sins and transgressions of the people against God?	24

The question is, What is behind the UFOs?

The results of the investigation with the psychic questionnaire may lead us to a plausible answer, one that will satisfy our curiosity and our growing spiritual concern.

Taken from the computer tabulation, the analysis of the questionnaire's relevant section — covering the major religious convictions and operations of those psychics who believe in UFOs — is extremely revealing.

Merely by singling out the replies to some of the most important religious questions included in the survey, and examining the answers given by those perpetrators of the supernormal who admit to practicing *all* its phenomena, it becomes clear that they do not share the belief of the average Christian. The psychics who believe in UFOs, advocate their importance, claim that they're inhabited by holy, sinless beings, and declare that Christ will return to earth in a UFO are the same people who also believe in communication with evil spirits; who look upon Christ as a superpsychic human being and believe that the devil is dead or at least, not very important. In addition, when measured by the tests of a "true prophet," someone who "speaks for God," they fail completely *by their own admission* — for the answers used above arc not those revealed by the circuitry of the PSE.

These people receive so-called godly revelations about the appearances and goals of the UFO beings. Can they possibly be on the side of God if they violate His guidelines?

If God does not inspire them in their psychic predictions concerning the activities and doctrines of the UFO beings, then who does? What's more, if, as we must conclude, their predictions are of satanic origin, how will this affect our belief in the phenomena we know as UFOs?

In their most recent predictions, the "prophets" have relayed their psychic impulses informing them of an imminent contact between people and the beings who control the UFOs.

One such predicted contact took place recently in a quiet residential section of Chattanooga, Tennessee, where a forty-three-year-old cabdriver had an experience he will not easily forget. Sitting in my car, tape recorder running, John Fuller told me of the intense fright that surged through him gray complexion, and humanlike hands with fingers looking like oilspouts.

"He kept assuring me that I would not be harmed, but I thought I was going to have a heart attack because of a explained apologetically, "but as I put my clothes on and rushed outside, I saw this light flashing at me from the sky . . . like a beacon or something going on and off . . . on and off . . .

"Then slowly the light drifted soundlessly toward me . . . toward Overman Street — "

I interrupted.

"Did it look like a space vehicle with lights? A helicopter? A balloon, perhaps?"

"I didn't see the vehicle," John countered. "All I saw was this severe light . . . you know, it scared me, for there was no noise . . . no sound, just that penetrating pulsating light, and suddenly I saw a figure standing on the righthand side of my driveway. Terrified, I started running back to the house, when the figure said, 'I am not here to harm you. You must come with me!' "

John stopped and wiped the perspiration from his forehead. It was a sweltering summer evening, and his nervousness about relating the event added to the heat.

"Suddenly I found myself inside the spacecraft," he continued, eyes focused on the running tape recorder. "It was large — you wouldn't believe how large. It goes beyond all imagination." And he proceeded to describe a spacecraft the size of a large football stadium, filled with gigantic wallpanels illuminated by myriad small, flashing lights. A soft humming sound could also be heard throughout the vehicle. Then his description centered on the inhabitants of the craft.

"There were six of them." John stopped and counted them over in his mind. "Five beside the leader who was with me. Five males and one female. They looked awfully strange to me." The leader (whom Fuller told me later was named "Ka-tel") was approximately seven feet, six inches tall, had a diamond-shaped head, triangular eyes, no nose, a bluish-when he was awakened at 1:45 Saturday morning, 5 July 1975, by an insistent flashing of a bright beam of light that illuminated his bedroom.

"At first I thought it was lightning or something," he

sudden severe pain in my chest. I was frightened, and it must have shown.

" 'You won't kill me, will you, you won't kill me?' I kept asking him, and suddenly he walked right over to me and touched me with his right hand. When he did that, all the pain and fright left me and I felt all relaxed. . . ."

Fuller, who told me he had been unable to sleep or eat since the incident, described a giant television-like screen mounted against one side of the spacecraft.

"Ka-tel turned to me," Fuller continued, "and said, 'Here is something you earth people are still uncertain about . . . you've guessed but will never really know the truth.' He walked over to the screen and suddenly the date of 22 November 1963 appeared in brilliant letters. Then there was a line of cars coming down a street. There was a close-up of a car. Connally was in the front seat and President Kennedy and his wife were in the back. Then it panned over a fence and showed a close-up of a man wearing white gloves and holding a high-powered rifle.

"It was Jack Ruby. He shot Kennedy in the neck and then placed the gun on the ground and walked into the parade section.

"I asked about Oswald, and it showed a scene of him sitting on some boxes in a building. He was trying to take aim but at first couldn't get the president in his sight. Then he shot him in the head. . . ."

With even more clarity, the beings produced a replay of the assassination of Dr. Martin Luther King, showing a bearded assassin again wearing white gloves.

"John, would you be willing to take a PSE test, a kind of lie-detector test, and let me discover whether you are really speaking the truth; whether this really happened to you?"

"Please, Mr. Noorbergen, please do. I want to know what happened to me. It's hard to believe. . . ."

Being prepared for the test, I had brought along a question form and quickly revised it to fit this bizarre interview. I then began asking the test questions.

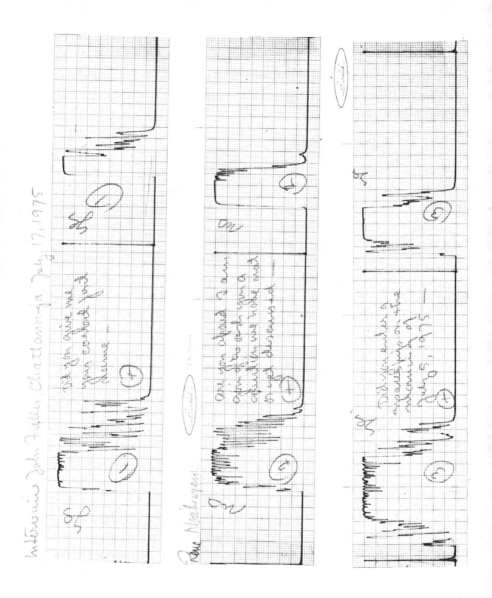

Figure 9. This graph and those on the following pages relate to John Fuller's description of an encounter with beings from a UFO.

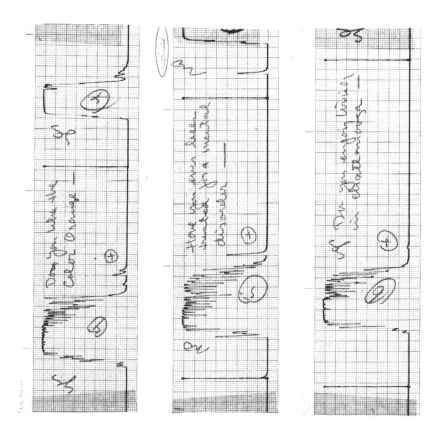

Figure 9a.

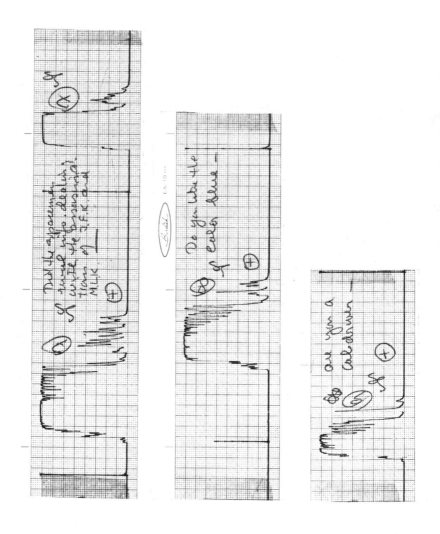

Figure 9b.

The Counterfeit

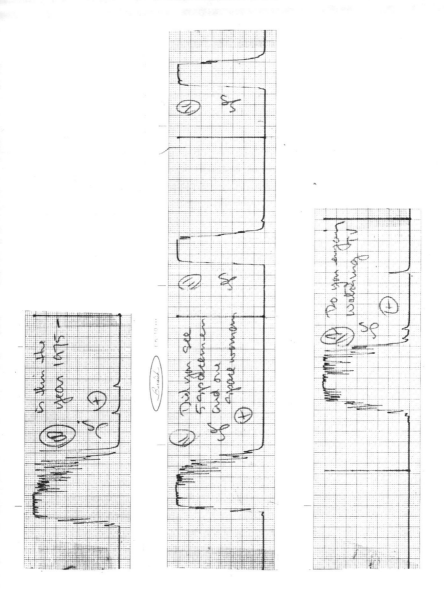

Figure 9c.

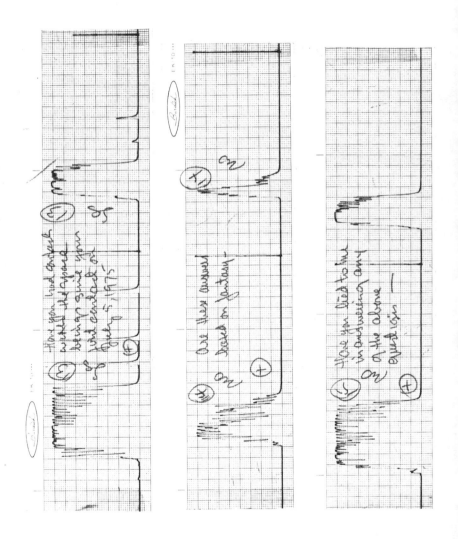

Figure 9d.

The Counterfeit

During that first interview with him, there was no doubt in my mind that he was frightened by his experience and wondering whether he might be going insane. Since that time, he has received several so-called telepathic contacts, impulses of a pending communication that reach him either at home or while driving his taxi, telling him that he has been chosen as a primary channel for space-to-earth communication.

Fantasy? Can it be solely an active imagination?

We thought so until the PSE interview was processed. The findings fully corroborated the Fuller account (figures 9-9d). I conducted a *second* test on Mr. Fuller, and he again cooperated voluntarily without any pressure from our side. Once more the results showed that John Fuller actually experienced something strange and unusual on the morning of 5 July 1975. Whether he was confronted with a visual sighting or whether a supernatural impression was imposed on his mind, we will never know. But something happened. The critical answers on the PSE test indicate a minimum amount of emotional stress, signifying a youthful response.

Today John Fuller is more than comfortable with his contacts.

"I hope they keep coming back to me as they have been doing for the rest of my life," the former Baptist church member told me. "I am beginning to enjoy these mysterious contacts, for they tell me they are willing to *help* us. I am certain now they are godly beings. . . ."

Godly beings . . . but are they really?

Let's examine the entire UFO phenomena from a religious aspect and make some pointed comparisons. We learn from various accounts that —

- the beings from the UFOs are seen and contacted via mediums and psychics.
- evil spirits forecast the appearances of UFOs.
- they claim that Christ's first coming was via a UFO.
- they predict that His second coming as a "cosmic master" will also be via a UFO.

165

— they inform us that the "evolution of mankind" is now being speeded up.

— according to them, reincarnation is a doctrine that has to be introduced.

— they insist the Bible has to be rewritten.

— they appear to be ugly, frightening, weird, and loathsome, just as they tend to appear in our imagination and science fiction.

— they create anxiety, terror, and tension.

These things we know they do. Equally as important to a Christian is what they fail to do. They don't —

— speak about the wonders of a holy society on their sinless planet;

— speak about the love of God;

— point toward an eternal life without the curse of sin;

— warn us, plead with us, to turn away from evil and accept Christ unreservedly;

— speak about the return of Christ soon as King of the world;

— come to us in fulfillment of a biblical prophecy forecasting their appearance in the time of the end.

There are strong indications that with UFOs we are confronted with satanic power. This premise is supported by the lack of genuine concern for the ultimate welfare of this fallen human race, as manifested by both the actions and doctrines of the UFO beings. We would expect holy visitors to express love and compassion, yet they instill fear. We would certainly expect them to help create a closer bond between us and our God, yet again they fail. All their elementary doctrines as relayed through the mediums are paganistic and self-serving. Christ commissioned His disciples to preach the gospel of the kingdom to the entire world to help our fellow-man. Should we not expect other heavenly beings to exhibit the same concern for mankind?

Angels felt great anxiety about the plight of the human race in biblical times. Proof of this can be found throughout both the Old and New Testaments. Should we expect them to act any differently now? Have we progressed that far on the way to perfection that heaven no longer cares?

In talking with theologians, I have not found even one who is willing to accept the premise that Satan was allowed to export sin beyond this planet, especially since Revelation 12:7-9 clearly speaks of his being cast down to earth — and nowhere else.

John says, "And there was war in heaven: Michael and his angels fought against the dragon; and the dragon fought and his angels, And prevaileth not; neither was their place found any more in heaven.

"And the great dragon was cast out, that old serpent, called the Devil, and Satan, which deceiveth the whole world: he was cast out into the earth, and his angels were cast out with him."

What then are these flying saucers?

To some people, the position that they are solely satanic manifestations may be a far-reaching proposition. But based on all available material on which to make our judgment, no other conclusion can be reached.

UFOs may well be a sophisticated, futuristic type of devilish manifestation.

Notes

[1]George King, *You Are Responsible* (London: The Aetherius Press, 1961), p. 81.
[2]Ibid., p. 151.
[3]Ibid., p. 113.
[4]Ibid., p. 117.
[5]Ibid., p. 118.
[6]*National Enquirer*, 5 December 1974.
[7]Ibid., 21 July 1974.

The Stars Don't Tell

7

7   The Stars Don't Tell

7 "WHEN THEY HAD HEARD THE KING, they departed; and, lo, the star, which they saw in the east, went before them, till it came and stood over where the young child was" (Matt. 2:9).

In all my years in journalism, I have never encountered such a well-concealed and well-contrived hoax as the one I uncovered through the application of the Psychological Stress Evaluator to the results of the Soul Hustlers Survey. There is no doubt in my mind now that a gigantic spiritual deception has been perpetrated on the human race, the true dimensions of which cannot as yet be ascertained.

It wasn't just the survey that convinced me, but it certainly reinforced my thinking.

Spiritualists now encompass us on all sides. They have successfully infiltrated the halls of government, scaled the otherwise unbreachable walls of the religious sanctuaries, and have even managed to capture the schools of the nation where the teaching of occult principles is becoming an increasingly common occurrence.

History has an odd way of repeating itself — but this is not the case with the development of psychic phenomena. It began as a mere whisper in the Garden of Eden and by now has evolved into a deafening crescendo of devilish laughter, increasing in force with each passing day.

"We've been taken over," a casual acquaintance of mine remarked when I showed him the initial results of the survey's computer printout. "What has happened to the influence of Christianity?"

The question is highly relevant. *What really has happened to the influence of Christianity?*

It is ironic that whereas the star of Bethlehem once heralded the greatest event of all time to the kings of the East, the stars are again thought to be the key to the secrets of tomorrow.

"They don't only forecast our future," I was told by one of the country's leading astrologers, "but they also guide us to the coming of a new Spiritual Master!"

Is there a possibility that they may be right? It is less than one hundred years from the religious awakening that stirred much of the country in the days of Moody to the world of 1976. But in that short span, the faith of Christ has been challenged increasingly by the faith of the Age of Aquarius — or as saucer-watcher George King prefers to call it, the faith of the Age of Aetherius.

Astrology as a forecasting tool has invaded millions of homes. As a result, most Americans no longer attend the church of their choice, simply because they have none . . . but ask them what they *do* believe in, and they'll tell you happily.

"Astrology and revelations are what we live by," they readily confess. "Spiritualism is our way of life. We follow the *new* way!"

Contrary to their understanding, the practice of astrology and psychic phenomena is as ancient as the stars from which it claims to reap its dubious knowledge. Primitive

The Stars Don't Tell

prophetic superstition has come a long way since the early pagans studied the liver of a sheep in order to find the magic key to the future. Known as hepatoscopy, this heathen method of divination was practiced extensively in old Babylonia. Looking into tomorrow's tomorrow by studying sheep intestines ran a close second in order of importance.

In modern society, however, prophecy by means of sheep entrails has little or no appeal. Now astrology is the accepted way. It is estimated that at the present time at least sixty million Americans live by the revelations of the stars. Borrowing *astra* and *logos*, meaning "star" and "word," from the ancient Greek, those who endorse *astro-logy* believe in the "word," the "revelation" that comes from the stars.

Astrology has a dark beginning, first seeing the light of day in pagan superstition in Mesopotamia, the land of the twin rivers, Euphrates and Tigris. It has been thought that it originated in that area as early as three thousand years before Christ. After the sixth century B.C., it then moved west toward Greece, where it developed into a prognosticative system seeming to have scientific merit. From Greece it traveled into the Roman Empire and Christian Europe, and finally, when Europe began to experience the strong influence of Islamic culture in the Middle Ages, this superstitious practice became fused with the Arabian influence, the result being modern astrology.

As a method for divining the future of kings and emperors, it slowly lost its eminence and nearly vanished from the political scene in the early nineteenth century.

Now, however, it has returned to chart the future of the common, everyday man at a time when we need it least of all!

Notwithstanding all the surveys, it is always difficult to determine the exact figures when trying to establish with any degree of accuracy the following of a certain cult. But the indications are that currently sixty million Americans now practice this ancient Mesopotamian divining method, relying on counsel and advice from ten thousand professional astrologers, more than two thousand astrology columns —

most of them advising on a day-to-day basis — and the hundreds of astrology magazines stacked at newsstands. Books on the subject are published at an increasing rate, and the vast variety of titles found on bookshelves give an inkling of the growing influence astrology has in every facet of American life.

Your Baby's First Horoscope and *Astrology for Teens* can be seen side by side with *Diet and Health Horoscope*, the *Cat Horoscope Book*, and *Cooking with Astrology*. Other books such as *Find Your Mate Through Astrology* and *Astrology and the Stock Market* are also reporting brisk sales. It is no wonder that membership in the astrological associations is at an all-time high.

It has been said that when future historians poke their fingers through the rubble of twentieth-century civilization, they will shake their heads in disbelief over so much organized confusion. For example, it has been reported that the Ford Motor Company consulted Charles A. Jayne, author of a horoscope column in the *New York Daily News*, to chart the future of the new Mustang automobile. Ridiculous as it may seem, Jayne's forecast was matched by the sales performance of the car.

"Those born September 21 [the introduction date of the car] are particularly endowed with the basic qualities of efficiency and resourcefulness," Jayne said. "Your moon in relation to Uranus indicates you are highly innovative and highly individualistic. Essentially, your planetary pattern is so well-balanced that you should be assured of a productive and successful life."

It was undoubtedly conceived as a public relations gimmick, but thousands believed in it and used the prediction as their basis for choosing a Mustang as their new mode of transportation.

Through this and other means, astrology has gained more over the years than it has lost. It is not unusual for many U.S. television stations to carry regularly scheduled astrology programs; just as others issue a twenty-four-hour weather forecast, one midwestern radio station now relays astrology forecasts several times a day.

Although it has been estimated that more women than men indulge in astrology's whims — the ratio is approximately four to one — it is not solely a woman's field. World War II historians tell us that during the height of the conflict, both the Nazis and the Allies consulted astrologers to help conduct the affairs of war. On the Nazi side, astrologers guided the decisions of men such as Heinrich Himmler, Rudolf Hess, and Adolf Hitler. Britain was not far behind. When the news of the activities of the Reich's astrologers reached London, Winston Churchill reacted by installing his own astrologer, Hungarian-born British Army Captain Louis de Wohl, who charted the stars and informed Churchill of the kind of decisions he might expect from the Germans. The unpredictable tides of war and the increasing battlefield losses eventually threw Hitler into a rage, and as a result, all of his astrologers were banished to the concentration camps.

Down through the ages, astrologers have had much to contend with. Even though the law of averages assures them a reasonable percentage of fulfilled predictions, their shortcomings and failures are so drastic and pronounced that they have prompted a number of ludicrous headlines. Jeane Dixon once predicted that Walter Reuther would be a candidate for the 1964 presidential election; he was not. Leading British astrologers predicted in 1939 that England would not be involved in a major war; when their prophecy backfired, they vainly attempted to rectify their mistake by saying that Hitler would fall within the year. Another monumental blunder occurred in April 1969 when most of the nation's astrologers warned that California — or at least a large portion of the state — would slip into the Pacific Ocean as the result of a devastating earthquake, similar in size to the one that ravaged San Francisco in 1906. Thousands of people abandoned the state, including Gov. Ronald Reagan, who left California that month for what was officially billed as a "planned vacation." But nothing happened. California is still there, and so are the astrologers.

Various astrologers have different PAQs (Prophetic Accuracy Quotients), but for a man who's accuracy is placed near the 75 percentile, British astrologer Maurice Woodruff's mistakes are too obvious to be ignored: Frank Sinatra and Mia Farrow would have a male child, he prophesied; the Vietnamese War would end practically overnight in April 1969; and Lynda Bird Johnson would tie the knot with George Hamilton. All these predictions would have made startling headlines if fulfilled, but all failed. Notwithstanding his failures, Woodruff was still regarded as one of the great astrologers. It seems that astrology buffs forgive easily.

The *Saturday Evening Post* commented in its February 1974 edition, "A survey of predictions by the three most popular British astrologers in one carefully monitored year showed one of them right only twelve out of thirty times, the second only nine out of thirty and the worst only four out of thirty tries."

If the ancients were not able to glean their supernatural knowledge from the stars (Dan. 2:27,28), and today we find our astrological prophets walking that same tightrope of unpredictability, then what is there in astrology that captures the minds of so many people? *What is it – and what's more, what are its governing principles?*

Let's take a quick look at the theoretical basis of this superstitious practice and see whether it makes any sense at all.

For every personal horoscope, the moment of birth is the essential starting point. This, coupled with the latitude and longitude of the individual's birthplace, provides the initial package for the usual astrological chart. While this is elementary, it is not complete; a factor known as "true local time" must also be considered. This "true" time is arrived at by adding or subtracting four minutes for each degree of longitude that your birthplace lies to the east or west of the center of your time zone of birth. Once this has been accomplished, the next step is to convert this "true" time into "sidereal" or star time. This is done with the aid of an ephemerus, a reference book showing the positions of the planets in relationship to the earth. Checking this star time in an astrological table is the last formal move, for in doing so, the theme of the individual's "ascendant" — the astrological sign that is supposed to have been rising on the eastern horizon at the moment of birth — is revealed.

Once you have developed this data — the experts tell me that these simple steps are no more difficult than solving a seventh-grade math problem — then you are ready to "chart" your horoscope. This means you align the "ascendant" with the nine-o'clock point on the inner circle of the horoscope, and from there you are prepared to "read" the various zodiacal "houses" that control your life and fortune. Granted, this is a simplified approach, and a few technical words and the names of the various houses have been omitted; however, the fundamental facts are there.

Astrology was an obscurity in the recesses of the Western mind prior to and during World War II, but with the emergence of an insatiable desire for knowledge of the supernatural, it soon outgrew its modern limitations and became the rage of the sixties. Even many people who frown on the practice of astrology more often than not know the "star sign" under which they supposedly were born.

As a result, the ten thousand professional astrologers are now united with millions of amateurs who chart their own horoscopes or have joined the ranks of those who frequent the several hundred horoscope computers currently in use at major department stores or airline terminals.

The question is, are they gaining anything besides satisfying the desires of a fatalistic view of life? Is there really something to astrology?

Many learned minds have dedicated their time, energy, and thoughts to solving this riddle of the ages and have come up with a variety of answers which, when combined, result in a devastating judgment against astrological superstition.

You may be certain of one thing: astrology does not depend on sound reasoning for its haphazard conclusions.

To believe in astrology, you must support the philosophy that you are either a "born loser" or a "born winner." The stars, we are being told, do not merely *forecast* the course of our lives, but they also *cause* the events to take place. They both *impel* and *compel*; they are a double fount of superstition.

Astrologers are usually easy to reason with and are more than willing to explain the principles with which they work — that is, until you face them with the six flaws in the structure of astrology. Within minutes, your friendly discussion will change into an antagonistic confrontation. By inserting these stingers into the defenses of the modern astrologers, you have opened Pandora's box and have thrust the crowbar of skepticism into their otherwise well-protected framework of superstition.

Astrology is a fair target for censure. First, *the geocentric theory is its basic flaw.*

Even though we live in a modern, technological society, ruled by scientifically supported data, the pseudoscience of astrology still rests on principles which were once thought to be universal, yet are now found to be rationally unacceptable.

Believing that the earth, not the sun, was the center of our planetary system, the ancient astrologers carefully based their predictive theory on the premise that we are all influenced by the planets that circled the earth. This geocentric idea originated about 3,000 B.C. and remained in force until Nicolaus Copernicus debunked it in A.D. 1540, approximately 4,500 years later. All heavenly bodies rotated, not around the earth, he discovered, *but the sun*. Everyone was under the assumption that we were the center, but with Copernicus' finding that we were only part of a *heliocentric* system and rotated around the sun like the other planets, astrology was dealt a crushing blow. It is bewildering enough to interpret the average horoscope, but what happens to its purported accuracy when the fundamental principles under-lying both prediction and interpretation are proven to be erroneous?

The second flaw in astrology is the *two-thousand-year-old near-sighted vision*. When reviewing the existing results, astrologers can no longer boast of 20/20 vision, for an obvious discrepancy has pervaded their predictive work. Copernicus created havoc in the astrologer's heavens when he disproved the theory of geocentricity, but that isn't all. Astronomers tell us that during the last two thousand years, the zodiac has shifted an entire "house" due to the gradual moving of the orbit of the sun through the stars. The sun has ceased to rise at zero degrees of the constellation Aries; now it seems to have traversed to a new location as far as seven degrees from Pisces. Even though this should be sufficient reason for the astrologers to rethink their figuring and have those born during the period of April 20 – May 20 reclassified as Gemini instead of Taurus, they still stubbornly stick to Taurus, for that is what the handbook says they should do. For them, superstition takes precedence over realistic changes. The fact that each house's calculation is off one complete month is of no concern to them.

Third is the fact that in astrology *there is no future above sixty-six degrees latitude*. Browsing through astrological charts and guidebooks for the do-it-yourselfer, one is astonished to find that a vital problem in astrology is conveniently ignored and overlooked. If there is one issue that needs answering, it is certainly the question of the sixty-six latitude.

It doesn't take long to realize that something is wrong with those living near the sixty-sixth degree latitude. They don't act or look different, but if we are to believe astrology, then we are faced with an enigma: at sixty-six degrees latitude it is nigh impossible to calculate precisely what con-stellation is rising on the horizon.

"Since we can't be sure which one is the right one at that point," one astrologer remarked to me in confidence, *"we cannot chart a horoscope for someone born in the Arctic regions.*

Areas like Finland, Greenland, Alaska, even northern Canada and other places are completely out of reach. . . ."

"Do you mean they are without a past or a future, astrologically speaking?" we wondered.

"Let's say that there is no evidence that their lives – or for that matter, their births – show any effect of the influence of the planets. Astrologically speaking, it is as if they had never been born."

It has been said that the most baffling thing in astrology is not drawing the horoscope, but interpreting it. Each horoscope, no matter who draws it, contains hundreds of disparate factors that can be interpreted many ways — all depending upon who does the analyzing. The experience and background of the astrologer are generally the guide for choosing or ignoring one or more of the divergent options available.

This policy works in most instances, but it leads us to question of *which twin has the future?* When dealing with fraternal twins, the curtain of uncertainty rises, and mental stagnation sets in. Reason compels us to assume that if two children are born perhaps a minute apart and join the human race under the same zodiacal sign, then their future lives must be nearly identical. Based on the laws and rules of astrology, they are influenced by the same planets and in addition have the same hereditary traits. The correlation between astrological futures should be extremely close — *yet it isn't.* Even though astrologers are almost forced by logic to draw the same horoscope for both individuals, they feel obliged to interpret the charts differently, because they are aware of the discrepancies that will occur should they issue the same forecast for both. They have learned through experience that no two lives are ever the same, and in the case of fraternal twins — those born at the same place and approximately at the same time — all astrological knowledge vanishes into pagan superstition.

There are, of course, other factors closely related to the problem of twins. When a plane crashes due to pilot error, are we then to believe that astrologically speaking this was the "preordained" time for all its passengers to die a fiery death? What about the thousands annihilated by the atomic bomb in Japan — can we really accept that instantaneously hundreds of thousands of different astrologically charted futures *had* to terminate the same day, in the same hour, in the same cruel, all-consuming minute?

Sometime ago I met a woman who had spent literally years of her life experiencing a "double-buying" sequence. As a child, whenever she bought a toy, invariably she purchased a second, identical one without knowing why. This happened with clothing, shoes, and other items. Finally, after puzzling many years over this oddity, she discovered that she was a twin; the other twin had died at an early age. The question that arises here, of course, is whether, astrologically speaking, she should have died with her sister, or whether her sister died in defiance of the wishes of the stars. . . . Who is right? Who is wrong? Astrology certainly does not have the answer, nor do we.

Then there is the astrological problem of the *influence of the "extra" planet*. Because of their limited scientific knowledge and the absence of the kinds of astronomical equipment we have today, the Mesopotamian priests were unable to make provision for uncharted planets that would someday be revealed through telescopes. Astrology has not changed noticeably since its inception, but the discovery of the planets Uranus, Neptune, and Pluto has greatly disturbed the tranquillity that once reigned among the astrologers. There simply was no place for these planets in the prophetic constellations. Many astrologers now conveniently blame the influence of these celestial bodies for some of the failures they have encountered in their forecasts. Inasmuch as they were never taught really to think for themselves — only to adhere to prescribed guidelines — having an "out" in case of a misinterpretation is extremely advantageous. Perhaps this is the rationale being used by astrologers like Criswell, who predicted that "hatching jackets" to protect expectant mothers from pain would be a big seller in the spring and summer of 1975 and that a one-hundred-dollar "instant cremation package" would be the rage of the day.

Others may use it to explain away the fact that the anticipated tidal wave of 10 April 1975 never materialized, leaving the "doomed sites" of Burma, Sumatra, India, Borneo, and Australia free of destruction!

— Last among astrological flaws is a trend toward belief in a superconsciousness of the planetary bodies. In their return to pure pagan concepts, astrologists are now advocating the idea that the solar system — both as a unit and in its separate parts — possesses oneness of consciousness and will and can beam this will at its discretion to influence and affect the affairs on earth . . . a superconsciousness that operates *without* God and *beyond* God. This is unquestionably a pantheistic view in which god-power is in everything and is a clear indication of astrology's pagan origin.

The results obtained through the Soul Hustlers Survey coincide strikingly with this conclusion. The telltale signs of astrology's heathen beginning appear as brilliant sparks of deception wherever the survey probes into the basis of the astrologer's faith. Only 28.6 percent of astrologers believe in the second coming of Christ; only 35.7 percent believe that Christ and Satan are engaged in what might be called "spiritual warfare"; less than half of all polled (42.9 percent) accept the Bible as God's valid guidebook; and even though 56.5 percent of them maintain that the world will end around the last year of this century, *only 14.3 percent see this happening simultaneously with the second coming of Christ.* Undoubtedly their feeling that Christ was only a superpsychic human being, *not* the Son of God, is partly responsible for this.

Throughout astrology, we find many indications reminding us that we are dealing with a pagan religion. Astrologers are cognizant of this and have seriously attempted to harmonize their practice with biblically approved methods of divination — without meaningful results.

God, however, does not compromise, and the Holy

Scriptures cannot be modified to meet the whimsical superstitions of modern pagan priests. The Lord's declarations about astrology have already been stated in chapter 3. The Bible does not accord astrology a place as a guiding beacon in the Christian community — but neither does the world of science.

The scientific testing of astrology has yielded perplexing results. However, the weight of evidence is not sufficient to erase all doubt, and on the other hand, it does not significantly support the basic premises of the astrologers. Coinciding with the rapid growth of modern astrology, protesting voices against its claims have arisen in the scientific community. Since astrology invades and contradicts the proud science of astronomy, it is expected that most of the objections would come from the astronomers. The predictions of the astrologers do not survive the experimental tests, for the practice of astrology operates illogically and beyond the realm of reason.

In 1949 the German Astronomical Society raised its head in protest. Renowned as one of the most respected scientific societies in the world, it denounced astrology as quackery, big business, and superstition. Other investigative committees, such as the 1949 Ghent University Committee (*Comité Belge pour l'investigation scientifique des phénomènes reputés paranormaux*) which listed thirty top ranking scientists as its members, concluded that the claims of the astrologers could not withstand the scientific test.

Yet, astrology continues to supplant the influence of Christianity on an ever-increasing scale. Perhaps this is why eighteen Nobel Prize winners and 186 prominent American scientists finally spoke out in September 1975 and blisteringly denounced the "pretentious claims of astrological charlatans," saying there is no scientific basis for widespread belief that the stars foretell events and influence lives.

The statement in a special issue of the *Humanists* magazine and carried worldwide through the wire services of the Associated Press said,

"This can only contribute to the growth of irrationalism and obscurantism. We believe the time has come to challenge, directly and forcefully, the pretentious claims of astrological charlatans."

The statement was originally drafted by Bart J. Bok, former president of the American Astronomical Society and professor emeritus at the University of Arizona.

"It is deplorable that so many newspapers now print this daily nonsense," Bok wrote in a separate article. "At the start, the regular reading is a sort of fun game, but it often ends up as a mighty serious business. The steady and ready availability of astrological predictions can over many years have insidious influence on a person's personal judgment."

Bok wrote that people believe in astrology because "in these uncertain times many long for the comfort of having guidance in making decisions. They would like to believe in a destiny predetermined by astral forces beyond their control. However, we must all face the world and we must realize that our futures lie in ourselves and not in the stars."

The statement said that astrology was part of the magical world view of the ancient people who had no concept of the distance from the earth to the stars and planets.

Now that these distances can and have been calculated, we can see how infinitesimally small are the gravitational and other effects produced by the distant planets and the far more distant stars. It is simply a mistake to imagine that the forces exerted by stars and planets at the moment of birth can in any way shape our futures.[1]

True Christianity cannot accept it; the Bible openly condemns it; the world of science blasts against its superstitious practices. But astrology moves on and gains impetus, guiding and directing the willing masses to a point in charted history where human destiny and the end of the world melt together into one calamitous event — the dissolution of mankind and the destruction of the world.

For many years — in fact since 1558, when the French astrologer Nostradamus published his now-famous prophetic guidebook called *Les Vrayes Centuries* (The True Centuries) — we have literally been inundated with prophecies leading us to the end of the world. Nostradamus achieved a high degree of accuracy, and among twentieth-century occultists his influence is still intensifying. His predictions forecasting the execution of Charles I of England by Parliament in 1649, the tumultuous events surrounding the French Revolution, the rise of the dictator Napoleon, and many other prophecies that found embodiment in political developments in both the nineteenth and twentieth centuries have placed him on the pedestal of astrological success. Never has there been an astrologer with such an astounding degree of prophecies fulfilled. A devout Catholic, he nevertheless accepted astrology as a God-ordained divining method, and because of the popularity his book has received within the last thirty years, his visions have been accepted by nominal Christians the world over.

Nostradamus might have gone unremembered as have many others were it not for his prophecy that the world would end within *our* lifetime.

Said he, in quatrain 10.72:

The year 1999, seventh month,
A Great king of terror will descend from
the skies.
To resuscitate the great king of Angolmois
Around this time Mars will reign for the
good cause.

Interpreters of this great seer's predictions claim that this signifies that the war-to-end-all-wars, the Battle of Armageddon, is to be fought in 1999, and victory will be on the side of those fighting for the good cause, because it will coincide with the coming of Christ and the end of the world as we know it today.

It may be a startling conclusion, but certainly not unique! The prophetic guideline that reaches us through the occult sciences has touched down on earth many times since the world began. Upon finding a susceptible medium, it invariably edges to predictions pointing toward the end of the world. Interestingly enough, this event is inevitably prophesied to transpire just prior to the year A.D. 2000.

When it concerns endtime predictions, many of our twentieth-century psychic seers and astrologers seem to have tapped into the same prophetic source as did Nostradamus. The late Edgar Cayce, the psychic who has attracted more followers in the last twenty years than any other prognosticator, looked far into the future and envisioned the destruction of the world preceded by global geological changes that were to commence in 1958 and continue for a period of approximately forty years. Every one of his forecasts dealing with this time period are threatening and condemnatory, but they all fuse into history at the climax of this forty-year span. That time, the year *1998*, Cayce predicted, "will be proclaimed as the period when His Light will be seen again in the clouds."[2]

Nostradamus and Edgar Cayce, however, are not the only seers who have clearly felt the effects of the end of days. Criswell, the Indiana-born psychic now living on the West Coast, continues to amaze his fans by repeatedly warning that we have just about reached the end of our civilization. He has so predicted that the end of the world will take place on *18 August 1999*, a slight refinement on the 1999 prophesied by Nostradamus in 1558.

Yet, when it comes to eloquence and power of description concerning this world's final days, no one seems more sincere and persuasive than Jeane Dixon. Among her voluminous predictions dealing with the extinction of mankind, she has forecast the appearance of a mysterious Child of the East who was born on 5 February 1962. This child, she claims, will he the answer to the prayers of the world. She sees his public emergence around the last decade of this century, and she is firmly convinced that the drama of the ages will indeed terminate before the year 2000, when a cross will appear in the eastern skies and a voice will ring out, echoing throughout the vast universe, saying, "Now ye are all my disciples." This, she believes, will coincide with the Battle of Armageddon and other catastrophic events.

Joey R. Jochmans of Creation History Research comments, "Many seers and psychics of today and of days gone by have identified the Middle Eastern child as a holy man and a possible Christ figure. Daniel Logan, who predicted a coming return to prominence for the Church, has also foreseen a similar rise to power of a child born in Egypt in 1962. Logan believes that a buried vault holding the secrets of ancient occult wisdom will soon be discovered in the child's homeland and that the child will utilize this wisdom in his world teachings.

"Another modern psychic, Alan Vaughan, has foreseen the advent of a holy man who will create a new religion that will supercede all other religions including Christianity."[3]

The Soul Hustlers Survey does not contain queries attempting to pin the occultists down to a specific *date* for the end of the world. But the question "Many psychics have predicted that the end of the world will come at the end of this century. Do you agree?" resulted in a meaningful response. Eighty percent of the psychic seers agreed on 1999; 75 percent of the faith healers endorsed it; and 56.5 percent of the astrologers agreed.

What is there about 1999 that seems to be so important? Why do more than half of the supernormal prognosticators believe that this is the year that will end all years? It is not a cheerful forecast, but it reappears with an inexplainable persistency. There must be a significant reason for the devil to keep inserting this prophecy into the psychic timetable.

Indeed there is! It is no secret that humanity is tired and worn out. The struggle between good and evil has endured longer than ever imagined by earlier generations, and promises of Christ's second coming become more appealing with each new crime statistic. The desire for peace is almost universal, and whosoever can guarantee the coming of a peacemaker will be held in great esteem. The pronouncements of the major psychics are speckled with predictions anticipating this wonder-worker; all are varied, yet all are the same — like different roads leading to the same city.

"It may well be asked just how plausible are these prophecies of a global union under one man?" responds Joey R. Jochmans. "The Christian world is awaiting the second coming of Christ, the Jews are looking for the Messiah, the Buddhists are seeking Maitreya, or the next Buddha, the Moslems are awaiting Muntazar, or the second Mohammed, and the Hindus look for Kalki, the next and last reincarnation of Vishnu in the flesh. Even small primitive hill tribes around the world are discarding their idols and are awaiting the appearance of an avatar or savior figure. If one man should stand up, particularly at a time when the world has gone through much warfare and destruction, and claims that he is each and every one of these expected saviours, the prophecies would become a certainty in no time."[4]

What is happening?

• Nostradamus expects the King of Terror to come down from heaven in July 1999.

• Edgar Cayce foresaw the end of wholesale geological destruction and the coming of Christ in 1998.

• Criswell has repeatedly stated that he foresees the end coming on 18 August 1999.

• Jeane Dixon sees the reign of a Child of the East followed by world peace in 1999.

Thus, according to the astrologers, a man of peace will begin his reign within the next twenty-four years. "It's in the stars," they tell us.

It may be their way of thinking, but is it biblical?

While both the Bible and secular prophecy do point toward a grand celestial event — the end of this world system combined with the return of Christ — God has not seen fit to disclose either the year or the day: "But of that day and hour knoweth no man, no, not the angels of heaven, but my Father only. . . . Watch therefore: for ye know not what hour your Lord doth come" (Matt. 24:36,42).

Mark 13:32,33 adds, "But of that day and that hour knoweth no man, no, not the angels which are in heaven, neither the Son, but the Father. Take ye heed, watch and pray: for ye know not when the time is."

The Bible simply does not announce the time reserved by God for the end of this world and the second coming of Christ. He undoubtedly has His own reasons for enshrouding this awe-inspiring climax in secrecy. *Yet, the psychics claim to know what had not even been revealed to the Son of God while He was on earth.* According to the majority of answers given in response to the Soul Hustlers Survey, most of the occult practitioners do not believe in the second coming of Christ, but rather in the mysterious appearance of an unbiblical "man of peace."

Because of this controversy, we are now confronted with an ultimate choice. With this prediction, are psychics telling us that we can relax and neglect all spiritual preparation for the next quarter-century and continue our way of life without concern for a possible *earlier* return of Christ? For those who persist in believing the psychics, it would be natural to accept the target date of 1999. Is this perhaps the crown on the Scheme of Grand Deception? Is its goal to lull us into forgetting Christ's admonition that no one "knows the day nor the hour" and then be found unprepared when He comes as a "thief in the night"?

Or is there a more sinister reason? For years the satanic agents have advised us of the arrival of this "loving" stranger who will eradicate all wrongs and open the door to a new tomorrow. We know from the Bible that the Antichrist is to make his appearance in the last days (Rev. 13:11-15). Can it be that as the final act of deception is played, Satan s forecasting his own entrance as Antichrist, to launch one last desperate attempt to rally humanity to his side just prior to the actual second coming of Christ? It is indeed comforting to look forward to the return of the man of peace, but must the announcements of His advent reach us through the pagan symbols of the stargazers and the senseless mutterings of satanically controlled mediums?

The groundwork for a mass deception has been laid — and laid well. By now, thousands of devil-inspired predictions have been fulfilled because of counterfeit-inspiration and the logical outcome of the law of averages. The entire system of satanic prophecy has been constructed in such a way as to lead us from the purity of biblical guidance into the maleficent clutches of the Prince of Darkness.

The disguise has been clever, but not beyond discovery. God forewarned us of satanic imitations of Christ in both the Old and New Testaments. Through the apostle Timothy we received an additional warning: "Now the Spirit speaketh expressly, that in the latter times, some shall depart from the faith, giving heed to seducing spirits, and doctrines of devils; Speaking lies in hypocrisy; having their conscience seared with a hot iron" (1 Tim. 4:1,2).

Both "seducing spirits" and "doctrines of devils" are now among us. But owing to the marvels of the electronic age, we have been permitted to eavesdrop on the innermost workings of the devil's mind. He has indeed *invaded* — not infiltrated — the Christian church, but his lying nature has been exposed, and his conscious efforts to deceive are now open to public scrutiny.

Notes

[1]New York: The Associated Press, 3 September 1975.
[2]Edgar E. Cayce, *Edgar Cayce on Atlantis* (New York: Paperback Library, Inc., 1968), pp. 158-59.
[3]Personal files.
[4]Ibid.